lonely planet

POCKET

BALI

TOP SIGHTS · LOCAL EXPERIENCES

T0022718

MASOVAIDA MORGAN, MARK JOHANSON, VIRGINIA MAXWELL

Contents

Participant at the procession before Nyepi (p22)
CRYSTAL IMAGE / SHUTTERSTOCK ©

Explore Bali   33

Survival Guide   145

COVID-19

We have re-checked every business in this book before publication to ensure that it is still open following the COVID-19 outbreak. However, the economic and social impacts of COVID-19 will continue to be felt long after the outbreak has been contained, and many businesses, services and events referenced in this guide may experience ongoing restrictions. Some businesses may be temporarily closed, have changed their opening hours and services, or require bookings; some unfortunately could have closed permanently. We suggest you check with venues before visiting for the latest information.

Special Features

Bali's Top Experiences

Explore Ubud's urban rice fields

Emerald patchworks blanket the land. **p114**

MARTIN PUDDY / GETTY IMAGES ©

GALITSKAYA / GETTY IMAGES ©

Get spiritual at Pura Luhur Ulu Watu

Bali's southernmost spiritual centre. **p80**

Soak up the sun on Kuta and Legian beaches

Get started at Kuta Beach: the birthplace of Bali tourism. **p36**

NITISH WALIA / SHUTTERSTOCK ©

Relax on laid-back Nusa Lembongan

Mellow escape to legendary sunsets. **p104**

Party till dawn on Gili Trawangan

Tropical playground with bohemian vibes. **p142**

ANDREW BROWNBILL / GETTY IMAGES ©

Dining Out

Bali's local cuisine, whether truly Balinese or influenced by the rest of Indonesia and Asia, draws from the bounty of fresh local foods and is rich with spices and flavours. Savour it at roadside warungs (simple cafes) or top-end restaurants. For tastes further afield, explore restaurants offering some of the best dining in the region.

Balinese Cuisine

The fragrant aromas of Balinese cooking will taunt you wherever you go. Even in your average village compound, the finest food is prepared fresh every day. Women go to their local marketplace first thing in the morning to buy whatever produce has been brought from the farms overnight and cook enough to last well into the evening. The dishes are covered on a table or stored in a glass cabinet for family members to serve themselves throughout the day.

Fast Food Bali-Style

Often, the most authentic Balinese food is found street-side. Locals of all stripes gather around simple food stalls in markets and on village streets, wave down *pedagang* (mobile traders) who ferry sweet and savoury snacks around by bicycle or motorcycle, and queue for *sate* or *bakso* (Chinese meatballs in a light soup) at the *kakilima* carts. *Kakilima* translates as something five-legged and refers to the three legs of the cart and the two of the vendor, who is usually Javanese.

Vegetarian Dreams

Bali is a dream come true for vegetarians. Tofu and tempe are part of the staple diet, and many tasty local favourites just happen to be vegetarian. Try *nasi saur* (rice flavoured with

HEDGEHOG111 / SHUTTERSTOCK ©

toasted coconut and accompanied by tofu, tempe, vegetables and sometimes egg), *urap* (a delightful blend of steamed vegetables mixed with grated coconut and spices), gado gado (tofu and tempe mixed with steamed vegetables, boiled egg and peanut sauce) and *sayur hijau* (leafy green vegetables, usually *kangkung* – water spinach – flavoured with a tomato-chilli sauce).

Bali's Best Restaurants

Bali Asli Ultra-fresh *nasi campur* and spectacular views over rice terraces are on offer at this hybrid restaurant and cooking school. (p140)

Mozaic A long-time fine-dining trend-setter in a lovely Ubud garden. (p127)

Hujon Locale Will Meyrick's stylish and casual farm-to-table eatery is emphatically and deliciously on-trend. (p123)

Bumbu Bali 1 A superb restaurant offering both exquisite dishes and well-regarded cooking classes. (p93)

Bar Open

Unlike other parts of Indonesia, Bali revels in drinking and nightlife. From coffee and fresh juices to the iconic Bintang beer and tropical cocktails, there's something to quaff for every taste and mood. Where to imbibe is even more varied: from beachside cafes to high-concept nightspots, you're never far from your next drink.

Beer & Wine

Beer drinkers are well catered for in Bali thanks to Indonesia's ubiquitous crisp, clean national lager, Bintang. Bali Hai beer sounds promising, but isn't.

Wine connoisseurs had better have a fat wallet. The abundance of high-end eateries and hotels has made fine vino from the world's best regions widely available but it is whacked with hefty taxes.

Medium-grade bottles from Australia go for US$50.

Local Booze

At large social gatherings, Balinese men might indulge in *arak* (fermented wine made from rice or palms or...other materials) but generally they are not big drinkers. Watch out for adulterated *arak*, which is rare but can be poisonous.

Fresh Juice

Local nonalcoholic refreshments are available from markets, street vendors, some warungs and many cafes. They

are tasty and even a little psychedelic (in colour) – and without the hangover! One of Bali's most popular drinks is *cendol,* an interesting mix of palm sugar, fresh coconut milk and crushed ice, with various other flavourings and floaties.

Coffee & Tea

Many Western cafes sell imported coffees and teas alongside local brands, some of which are very good.

The most expensive (and most overhyped) coffee is Indonesia's

peculiar *kopi luwak*. Around 200,000Rp a cup, it's named after the catlike civet (*luwak*), indigenous to Sulawesi, Sumatra and Java, that feasts on ripe coffee cherries. Entrepreneurs initially collected the intact beans found in the civet's droppings and processed them to produce a supposedly extra-piquant brew. Now that interest in *kopi luwak* has exceeded all reason, trouble abounds, from fraudulent claims to documented animal mistreatment.

Best Beach Clubs

Omnia Bali's hottest southernmost day club blasts hip-hop beats over the cliffs of the Bukit peninsula. (p86)

Potato Head It doesn't get any more stylish than this multilevel lounge and venue right on the beach. (p68)

La Plancha Bask under coloured umbrellas on the sand before the DJ gets the beach party started. (p57; pictured)

Best Partying

La Favela Through Bali's most alluring entrance, you'll find a bar filled with boho fun. (p55)

Jenja Slick, multilevel nightclub with well-heeled locals and expats. (p46)

Best Coffee

Revolver Retro, Wild West–inspired coffee bar with stellar brews and bites. (p57)

Bhineka Djaja Locally grown beans and a mean espresso on Denpasar's old main drag. (p110)

Treasure Hunt

Some consider Bali a great destination for shopping; for others it's their destiny. With designer boutiques (Bali has a thriving fashion industry), slick galleries, wholesale emporiums and family-run workshops, Bali's shops could occupy days of your holiday.

Seminyak's Shops

Shopping in Seminyak and Kerobokan is reason enough to visit Bali – the choice is extraordinary. Along with countless open-air markets selling typical Balinese treasures like rattan handbags and sarongs, there are surf shops, fashion boutiques and jewellery designers galore.

Shopping Ubud

Ubud is home to art shops, boutiques and galleries. Many offer items that have been made locally. There's also an enormous number of craft galleries, studios and workshops in villages north and south.

The area's main shopping strip has moved to Jl Peliatan in Tebesaya and Peliatan. Here you'll find all the stores and shops that supply locals with their daily needs.

Bargaining

Bargaining can be an enjoyable part of shopping in Bali. Try following these steps:

○ Have some idea of the item's worth.

○ Establish a starting price – ask the seller for their price.

○ Your first offer can be from one-third to two-thirds of that price.

○ If you don't like the price, walk – the vendor may go lower.

○ When you name a price, you're committed – you must buy if your offer is accepted.

Best Fashion

Bamboo Blonde Chain of cheery local-designer boutiques. (p59)

Thaikila Balinese-made bikinis, with a soupçon of French style. (p57)

AMNAT30 / SHUTTERSTOCK ©

Uma & Leopold Luxe threads and little frilly things to put on before slipping off. (p58)

It Was All A Dream Hip boutique with quality leather goods, vintage denim and jersey basics. (p71)

Best for Browsing

Love Anchor Hipster market in a traditional *joglo* setting. (p70)

Ganesha Bookshop Bali's best bookshop has carefully chosen selections. (p131)

Pasar Badung This large central market has it all. (p111; pictured)

Theatre Art Gallery Vintage and replica puppets. (p58)

Best Homewares

Souq Inspired by the Middle East, designed in Bali. (p58)

Kou Handmade soaps bring the evocative scents of Bali home with you. (p130)

Namaste The place to buy a crystal to get your spiritual house in order. (p132)

Best for Surfers

Dylan Board Store Custom boards by noted surfer Dylan Longbottom. (p71)

Drifter Surf Shop High-end surf wear. (p57)

Luke Studer Renowned south Bali board shaper. (p47)

Surfer Girl Another of Bali's iconic surf brands. (p47)

Best Gifts & Souvenirs

Threads of Life Indonesian Textile Arts Center Handmade traditional Bali fabrics. (p130)

Joger A Bali retail legend. (p47)

Ashitaba Beautiful, ornate rattan work. (p59)

Confiture de Bali Sweet boutique selling butters and jams made from local fruits. (p133)

Beaches

Bali is ringed with beaches, which come in so many forms that there's a perfect patch for everyone. There's a reason that tourism started in Kuta: just look at that beach. It disappears in both directions and has ceaselessly crashing waves, which at their best are long aqua ribbons twisting into white.

A Beach for Every Mood

On Sundays Kuta Beach is thronged with locals; on any day massages and cheap beers from coolers are offered along the beach. Holidaymakers claim a part of the beach they like, make friends with the vendors and return to 'their' beach for the rest of their trip. From Seminyak north through Batubelig, Batu Bolong and on to Echo Beach, hipster hang-outs vie with posh clubs and humble beer vendors for business.

South of the airport, the vast arid rock that is the Bukit peninsula shelters a score of beaches hidden in small coves below the cliffs all the way to Ulu Watu. Coming closest to the white-sand cliché, these idylls are good for watching the world-class surfing offshore amid beautiful surrounds. Meanwhile, in Nusa Dua, Tanjung Benoa and Sanur, families frolic on mellow reef-sheltered beaches picked clean daily. East Bali has a swath of seldom-visited volcanic black-sand

beaches, while Nusa Lembongan has beach guesthouses with awesome sunset views. Over on Gili T, the sand is white and lined with bars and clubs for a full-on party scene.

Best for Hanging with Friends

Double Six Beach Fun mix of visitors and locals. (p40)

Gili Trawangan Those raves about the raves are just the start. (p142)

Seminyak Beach Clubs and cafes great and humble dot the sand. (p52)

Batu Bolong Beach Hot spot with a cool, all-inclusive scene. (p65)

MICHELE FALZONE / GETTY IMAGES ©

Balangan Beach Classic cove beach – worth the trek. (p83; pictured)

Kuta Beach The original beach still knows how to kick up some sand. (p36)

Echo Beach Wicked surf action entertains the masses. (p65)

Padang Padang Beach Small enough to be one big scene on busy days. (p83)

Best for Families

Kuta Beach Great surf schools. (p36)

Sanur Beach Kids will get their kicks in the gentle surf. (p100)

Batu Bolong Beach Where the cool kids of all ages hang out. (p65)

Best for Escaping

Bingin Beach Difficult access makes this spot not to be spotted. (p84)

Pantai Patra Jasa A hidden gem near the airport. (p40)

Best for Chilling Out

Balangan Beach This curving white-sand beach is ramshackle in an endearing way and perfect for a snooze or booze. (p83)

Nusa Lembongan Beaches Little coves of dreamy sand you can walk between, plus fab swimming. (p104)

Best for Beach Dining

Jimbaran Famous for its array of beachside restaurants serving grilled seafood. (p75)

Pasir Putih Near Candidasa White Sand Beach is the coolest beach in east Bali, with great cafes. (p135)

Pantai Lebih Admire fishing boats along the shore as you sample the catch of the day. (p139)

Diving & Snorkelling

With warm water, extensive reefs and abundant marine life, Bali offers excellent diving and snorkelling. Reliable dive schools and operators around the island can train complete beginners or arrange challenging trips that will satisfy the most experienced divers.

Best Sites

Bali's most spectacular diving and snorkelling locations draw people from near and far. Skilled divers will enjoy the challenges of Nusa Penida, as well as the schools of manta rays and 2.5m sunfish, but novices and snorkellers will be in over their heads. Spectacular 30m walls await off Pulau Menjangan and are good for divers and snorkellers of all skills and ages. Tulamben (p140), with its sunken WWII freighter, is another site for both divers and snorkellers with good swimming skills.

Equipment

If you're not picky, you'll find all the equipment you need in Bali, the Gilis and Lombok (the quality, size and age of the equipment can vary). If you bring your own, you can usually get a discount on your dive.

Some small, easy-to-carry things to bring from home include protective gloves, spare straps, silicone lubricant and extra globes/bulbs for your torch. Tanks and weight belts are usually included in the cost of the dive.

Other equipment to consider bringing includes a mask, snorkel and fins; a thin, full-length wetsuit (if diving off Nusa Penida, you'll need a wetsuit thicker than 3mm, as up-swells bring up 18°C water from the deep); and regulators and BCVs.

DUDAREV MIKHAIL / SHUTTERSTOCK ©

Best Diving

Gili Trawangan Dive shops and spots abound on Gili T. Free-diving is popular here, and there are reefs in all directions. (p142)

Nusa Lembongan There are dozens of great sites here and at the two neighbouring islands. (p104)

World Diving This excellent Nusa Lembongan operator leads trips and offers certification. It also organises trips to the deep and challenging waters off nearby Nusa Penida. (p105)

Crystal Divers Sanur's top dive shop gives great lessons and organises trips. (p101)

Best Snorkelling

Gili Trawangan Wander into water teeming with fish and reefs right off the beach. (p142)

Nusa Lembongan Reefs and mangroves combine for many fine sites. (p104)

Padangbai Have fun snorkelling right off the beach. (p140)

Surya Water Sports (☎0361-287956; www.balisuryadivecenter.com; Jl Duyung 10; ⏱8am-8pm) Sanur's best water-sports shop offers boat trips for snorkellers.

Under the Radar

One of the great delights and surprises Bali is the ease with which you will be able to head off the tourist track. Away from the coast or from central Ubud, tranquil temples, emerald-green rice fields and mountain villages dot the hinterland, providing plenty of opportunities for rewarding day trips or relaxing overnight breaks.

Temple Visits

Most visitors to Bali have been lured by the siren call of its legendary beaches, but it is true to say that these glorious stretches of white sand garlanding the southern coastline can be unpleasantly crowded for many months of the year. To escape the madding crowd, consider visiting one of the many temples in the centre of the island, where the daily rituals of work and worship unfold amid a lush landscape dominated by volcanoes and hillside rice terraces.

Take a Walk

Yes, you can zoom around on a motorcycle or catch a wave on a surfboard. But one of the best ways to get moving on Bali is to explore on foot. If you take this option and head into fields and villages away from the coast, you will get a feel for the appreciably slower and more spiritual pace of life embraced by locals elsewhere on the island.

Best Temples

Gili Trawangan Dive shops and spots abound on Gili T. Free-diving is popular here, and there are reefs in all directions. (p142)

Pura Lempuyang Panoramic views from seven temples perched on a steep mountain slope. (p137)

Pura Besakih Bali's most important Hindu temple complex is located on Gunang Agung, an active volcano. (p137)

Pura Taman Saraswati Honouring the Hindu goddess of wisdom and the arts, this water temple in Ubud is pretty as a picture. (p121)

EDMUND LOWE PHOTOGRAPHY / SHUTTERSTOCK ©

Best Walks

Sidemen Village Set on a hilltop rising out of a river valley, this rural village has tranquility and beauty in equal measure. (p140; pictured)

Ubud's Urban Rice Fields Listen to a symphony of frogs, birds and gurgling water as you walk through emerald-green paddy fields. (p114)

Batubelig to Pererenan This 4km walk passes a lagoon, fishing huts and a temple. Dozens of great sites here and at the two neighbouring islands. (p162)

Top Tips

Set in the misty jungle terrain of the Central Mountains, the village of Munduk doesn't feature in many Bali travel itineraries, but those who make the trek here are rewarded by blissfully cool breezes, views down to the island's northern coast and a terrain dotted with tumbling waterfalls. The Dutch planters who established coffee and spice operations here also constructed summer homes, many of which now function as guesthouses, so this is an idyllic spot to escape the coastal crowds and enjoy a few days of hiking from waterfall to waterfall.

Pampering

Whether it's a fix for the mind, body and spirit, or a desire for serenity, visitors to Bali spend many happy hours (sometimes days) being massaged, scrubbed, pampered, bathed and blissed out. Sometimes this attention to your well-being happens on the beach or in a garden, other times it's in stylish, even lavish, surroundings.

LUCKY BUSINESS / SHUTTERSTOCK ©

Pick Your Bliss

Spas may be serious or they may seem frivolous; they can be found down little lanes and in the most exclusive hotels. Treatments are myriad, from the almost sensually relaxing to serious endeavours designed to purge your body and maybe your soul of toxins. You can lie back and enjoy or take active part; yoga is hugely popular. Happily the Balinese have just the right cultural background and disposition to make it a truly revitalising experience.

Balinese Massage

Traditional Balinese massage techniques of stretching, long strokes, skin rolling and palm and thumb pressure result in a lowering of tension, improved blood flow and circulation, and an all-over feeling of calm. Traditional herbal treatments are also prevalent; it's the perfect holiday prescription.

Best Massage

Jari Menari Bali's renowned centre for serious massage. (p53)

Sundari Day Spa Organic massage oils set the mood at this day spa. (p66)

Best Spas

Jamu Traditional Spa Popular, serene and posh. (p42)

Jamu Wellness Classy establishment with a range of treatments. (p101)

Best Yoga

Yoga Barn The centre for all things yoga in Ubud. (p123)

Taksu Spa Combines yoga with spa treatments. (p123)

Power of Now Oasis Beachside yoga at dawn. (p100)

Surfing

TRUBAVIN / SHUTTERSTOCK ©

On Bali you have dozens of great breaks in each direction. This was the first place in Asia where surfing took off and, like the perfect set, it shows no signs of calming down. Surfers buzz around the island on motorbikes with board racks, looking for the next great break. Don't miss classic surfer hangout Balian Beach.

Where to Surf

Swells come from the Indian Ocean, so the surf is on the southern side of the island and, strangely, on the northwest coast of Nusa Lembongan, where the swell funnels into the strait between there and the Bali coast.

In the dry season (around April to September), the west coast has the best breaks, with the trade winds coming in from the southeast; this is also when Nusa Lembongan is at its best. In the wet season, surf the eastern side of the island, from Nusa Dua around to Padangbai. If there's a north wind – or no wind at all – there are also a couple of breaks on the south coast of the Bukit peninsula.

To reach the breaks, many will rent a motorbike with a surfboard rack while others will hire a surfboard-carrying-capable car with a driver. Either option is easily accomplished.

Best Surf Breaks

Kuta Beach Bali's first surf beach is still a winner. (p36)

Batu Bolong Beach Light sand, lots of surfers and a cool party scene. (p65)

Bingin Close to cheap surfer lodgings, this isolated beach is worth the climb down a cliff. (p84)

Double Six Beach Great mix of tourists and locals. (p40)

Impossibles Challenging outside reef break. (p84)

Echo Beach Wild waves and plenty of spectators. (p65)

Ulu Watu Bali's best surf breaks are truly incredible. (p83)

Balangan Right off a great beach with fun cafes. (p83)

Nusa Lembongan Three famous breaks are right off Jungutbatu Beach. (p104)

Festivals & Events

There you are, sitting in a cafe when there's a crash of the gamelan and traffic stops, elegantly dressed people bearing fruit, parasols and a masked Barong (mythical lion-dog creature) passing by. It's a temple procession, disappearing as suddenly as it appeared, leaving no more than hibiscus petals in its wake. Dozens occur daily.

MARIO ANDI SUPRIA / SHUTTERSTOCK ©

Offerings to the Gods

No matter where you stay, you'll witness women making daily offerings around their family temple and home, and in hotels, shops and other public places. You're also sure to see vibrant ceremonies, where whole villages turn out in ceremonial dress, the roads closed for a spectacular procession that can stretch for hundreds of metres. There's nothing manufactured about what you see. Performances at hotels are among the few events 'staged' for tourists, but they do actually mirror the way Balinese traditionally welcome visitors.

Best Special Days

Nyepi The year's most special day is marked by total inactivity – to convince evil spirits that Bali is uninhabited, so they'll leave the island alone. The night before, huge papier-mâché monsters (*ogoh-ogoh*) go up in flames. You'll see these built by enthusiastic locals in communities islandwide in the weeks before. Held in March or early April.

Galungan One of Bali's major festivals. During a 10-day period, all the gods come down to earth for the festivities, which celebrate the death of a legendary tyrant called Mayadenawa. Barong prance from temple to temple and village to village (many of these processions consist entirely of children), and locals rejoice with feasts and visits to families. Dates vary greatly as the 210-day *wuku* (or Pawukon) calendar is used to determine festival times.

Kuningan (pictured) Culmination of Galungan, when the Balinese say thanks and goodbye to the gods. You'll see large temple ceremonies across the island – and likely be caught in long traffic queues as a result. Abandon your vehicle and join the scene. On beaches, families dressed spotlessly in white look for purification from the ocean's waters.

Art

Until visitors arrived on Bali in great numbers, painting or carving were purely to decorate temples and shrines and enrich ceremonies. Today, with galleries and craft shops everywhere, canvases are stacked up on gallery floors and you may trip over carvings in both stone and wood. Amid the tat, however, you'll find beautiful work.

IMAGEMORE CO. LTD / GETTY IMAGES ©

Painting

Balinese painting is probably the art form most influenced by Western ideas and demand. Traditional paintings, faithfully depicting religious and mythological subjects, were for temple and palace decoration. In the 1930s Western artists introduced the concept of paintings as artistic creations that could also be sold for money. The range of themes, techniques, styles and materials expanded enormously, and women painters emerged for the first time.

Crafts

Bali is a showroom for crafts from around Indonesia. Nicer tourist shops sell puppets and batiks (pictured) from Java, ikat garments from Sumba, Sumbawa and Flores, and textiles and woodcarvings from Bali, Lombok and Kalimantan. The kris (traditional dagger), important to a Balinese family, will often have been made in Java.

Best Museums & Galleries

Museum Le Mayeur House and gallery of one of Bali's most influential painters. (p99)

Agung Rai Museum of Art Excellent private museum in Ubud. (p120)

Museum Puri Lukisan A great history of Balinese art. (p120)

Pasifika Museum Large museum with fine works from Bali and the region. (p91)

Neka Art Museum Has paintings by many of the local greats. (p120)

Museum Negeri Propinsi Bali The island's main museum has art from across the ages. (p109)

For Kids

MATT MUNRO / LONELY PLANET ©

Travelling with anak-anak (children) in Bali is an enriching experience. Locals consider kids part of the community, and everyone has a responsibility towards them. Children of all ages will enjoy both the attention and the many diversions that will make their holiday as special as that of the adults.

The Balinese & Children

Children are a social asset when you travel in Bali, and people will display great interest in any Western child they meet. You will have to learn your child's age and sex in Bahasa Indonesia – *bulan* is month, *tahun* is year, *laki-laki* is boy and *perempuan* is girl. You should also make polite enquiries about the other person's children, present or absent.

Best Regions for Kids

Kuta & Legian Though it's crowded and crazy here, beachfront resorts, surf lessons and all manner of cheap souvenirs will entice kids and teens. (p35)

Nusa Dua Huge beachside resorts with kids programs, a reef-protected beach and modest traffic. (p89)

Sanur Beachside resorts, a reef-protected beach, light traffic and proximity to many kid-friendly activities. (p95)

Ubud There are many things to see and do (walks, monkeys, markets and shops).

Evenings may require greater creativity to keep younger kids amused, although many will be entranced by the dance performances. (p113)

Best Watery Fun

Kuta Beach Surf schools. (p36)

Sanur Beach Kids will get their kicks in the gentle surf. (p100)

Batu Bolong Beach Where the cool kids of all ages hang out. (p65)

Waterbom Park A huge aquatic playground. (p41)

LGBTIQ+

Bali ranks as one of the world's most tolerant LGBTIQ+ travel destinations. Much of this stems from Balinese beliefs and attitudes. People are accepted as they are, judging others is considered extremely rude, and macho culture is generally limited.

ALEXANDER_H_SCHULZ / GETTY IMAGES ©

Bali & LGBTIQ+ Travellers

Bali has a large gay and lesbian expat community and many own businesses that – if not gay-specific – are very gay-friendly. In south Bali and Ubud, couples have few concerns, beyond remembering that the Balinese are quite modest. Otherwise, there's a strip of very-gay-friendly nightclubs in the heart of Seminyak, although there's no part of Bali any LGBTIQ+ person should avoid.

Having said that, gay travellers in Bail should follow the same precautions as heterosexual travellers and avoid public displays of affection.

Best LGBTIQ+ Nightlife

Bali Joe Fab drag shows draw a mixed crowd; several other clubs are nearby. (p57)

Top Tips

○ Gay men in Indonesia are referred to as homo or gay; lesbians are *lesbi*.

○ Indonesia's transvestite and transsexual *waria*, from the words *wanita* (woman) and *pria* (man), have always had a public profile.

○ **GAYa Nusantara** (www.gayanusantara.or.id) covers local LGBTIQ+ issues and **Gaya Dewata** (www.gayadewata.com) is Bali's gay organisation.

Four Perfect Days

Day 1

Start your tour of the island in the place where tourism in Bali began. Learn to surf at **Rip Curl School of Surf** (p41), then join late-risers and all-night clubbers for lunch on the north end of Legian: try either **Warung Asia** (p43) or **Warung Murah** (p43).

In the afternoon catch some beach action at **Kuta Beach** (p37; pictured), **Legian Beach** (p37) or **Double Six Beach** (p40).

After sunset enjoy an elegant meal at **Poppies Restaurant** (p44) or **Fat Chow** (p44) before the all-night party march. Make **Sky Garden Lounge** (p46) your hub, with forays to surrounding venues.

Day 2

Head east through lush foot-hills to Ubud, where you can have a healthy lunch at **Moksa** (p124) or something more traditional at **Nasi Ayam Kedewatan** (p123). Seek serenity at **Yoga Barn** (p123) or **Taksu Spa** (p123), or do it yourself with a walk through Ubud's **rice fields** (p114; pictured).

Catch a **traditional dance show** (p129) and see dancers go through precise motions to the cacophony of the gamelan (traditional orchestra).

For dinner, try **Locavore** (p127) or one of many good places on Jl Dewi Sita.

Day 3

DOLLY MJ / SHUTTERSTOCK ©

Using Sanur as your hub, begin the day with a market run in Denpasar at **Pasar Badung** (p111; pictured) – selections are freshest in the morning. Join locals for a cooked-to-order lunch at **Depot Cak Asmo** (p110) before heading back to lay low for a bit on **Sanur Beach** (p100).

Pull yourself up from the sand and swing up to the rice fields and lush green hills along the Sidemen Road. Get in some spa time at **Jamu Wellness** (p101) or shopping at **A-Krea** (p103) for Bali-designed goods.

Feast on fresh grilled seafood at **Char Ming** (p102) for dinner.

Day 4

CHEECHEW / SHUTTERSTOCK ©

Check out Jimbaran's **fish market** (p75) early, then head to the **Pasifika Museum** (p91) to behold relics by the Balinese and other Pacific cultures.

Next, have lunch at **Single Fin** (p87), where you can enjoy hypnotic swells with your poke bowl from a clifftop perch.

Head to **Pura Luhur Ulu Watu** (p80) for sunset and the **dance performance** (p87; pictured) that follows, then dinner at **Bumbu Bali 1** (p93).

Need to Know

For detailed information, see Survival Guide p145

Currency
Rupiah (Rp)

Languages
Bahasa Indonesia and Balinese

Visas
Easily obtained; can be a hassle for stays longer than 30 days.

Money
ATMs and money exchange counters are common. Credit cards are accepted at upmarket establishments.

Mobile Phones
Local SIM cards (from 5000Rp) are sold everywhere. Expect data speeds of 3G and faster.

Time
Indonesia Central Time (GMT/UTC plus eight hours)

Tipping
A set percentage is not expected; 5000Rp or 10% or more is appropriate for exceptional service.

Daily Budget

Budget: Less than US$80

Room at guesthouse or homestay: less than US$50

Cheap food and drink, meals: under US$5

Beaches: free

Midrange: US$80–250

Room at midrange hotel: US$50–150

Great night out eating and drinking: US$20+

Spa treatment: US$10–40

Top end: More than US$250

Room at top-end hotel or resort: US$150+

Lavish evening out: US$40+

Car and driver per day: US$60

Useful Websites

Bali Advertiser (www.baliadvertiser.biz) Excellent columns with info for visitors.

Bali Discovery (www.balidiscovery.com) The weekly online news report is a must-read of events in Bali.

The Beat Bali (http://thebeatbali.com) Useful website and twice-weekly publication with extensive entertainment and cultural listings.

GU Guide (https://cangguguide.com) Female-run website highlighting the hippest happenings in Canggu.

Ubud Now and Then (http://ubudnowandthen.com) Ubud-centric info and features as well as excellent Bali-wide cultural listings.

The Yak (www.theyakmag.com) Glossy, cheeky mag celebrating the expat swells of Seminyak and Ubud.

Arriving in Bali

✈ Ngurah Rai International Airport

Ngurah Rai International Airport (http://bali-airport.com), just south of Kuta, is the only airport in Bali. It is sometimes referred to internationally as Denpasar (it's located 13km south of the city) or on some internet flight-booking sites as Bali.

Bali's current airport terminal opened in 2013. Unfortunately, it has many problems, including outrageous food and drink prices, a serpentine layout and long lines at immigration and customs.

International airlines flying to and from Bali have myriad flights to Australia and Asian capitals. The present runway is too short for planes flying nonstop to/from Europe.

Getting Around

The best way to get around is with your own transport, whether you drive, hire a driver or cycle. This gives you the flexibility to explore places that are otherwise inaccessible.

🚗 Car

Rent a small 4WD for under US$30 a day or get a car and driver for US$60 a day.

🚲 Motorbike

Rent one for as little as US$5 a day.

🚐 Public Transport

Bemos (minibuses) provide very cheap transport on fixed routes but are very infrequent and hard to find.

🚕 Taxi

Fairly cheap, but only use Bluebird Taxis to avoid scams.

Bali Regions

Ubud (p113)
Bali's cultural heart is an alluring mix of creative boutiques, spas and cultural performances.

Ubud's Urban Rice Fields 👁

Kerobokan & Canggu (p61)
Villas and surfer guesthouses mingle with rice fields and fine dining. Beaches range from lonely to trendy; the waves here are bigger than further south.

Denpasar (p107)
Bali's sprawling, chaotic capital is the island's population hub. Look for museums and monuments, plus vibrant shopping and eating.

Seminyak (p49)
Streets lined with designer boutiques and shops of every sort: oodles of good restaurants, and the beach is never far away.

Kuta & Legian Beaches 👁

Kuta & Legian (p35)
Bali's chaotic heart of mass tourism has squawking vendors and sweaty clubs all jammed in tight against a legendary beach.

Pura Luhur Ulu Watu 👁

Ulu Watu (p79)
Pocket-sized white-sand beaches sit in coves below cliffs. Bamboo cafes cater to surfers and their fans.

Jimbaran (p73)
A low-key bay and beach; the action is at the famous fish market and dozens of beachside grilled-seafood joints.

Sanur (p95)
Combines Balinese style with a thriving expat community. The quiet beach is perfect for families too mature for Kuta.

Nusa Lembongan

East Bali (p135)
In the shadow of Gunung Agung, Bali's most important volcano, enjoy black-sand beaches, historic sights and impossibly green vistas.

Nusa Dua & Tanjung Benoa (p89)
Fronted by a reef-protected beach, Nusa Dua is a gated top-end resort world, while Tanjung Benoa caters to midrange groups.

Explore
Bali

Bali's Walking Tours 🥾

Worth a Trip 🔭

Local women carrying offerings to a village temple, Ubud (p113)
CHEN WS / SHUTTERSTOCK ©

Explore ✥

Kuta & Legian

Loud and frenetic, Kuta and Legian are the epicentre of mass tourism in Bali and often the first place many visit; however, the region isn't for everyone. Kuta has narrow lanes jammed with cheap cafes and T-shirt vendors, though flash malls and chain hotels indicate a growing consumer culture. Legian appeals to a slightly older crowd — it's equally commercial and has many family-friendly hotels close to the beach.

The Short List

○ **Kuta Beach (p37)** *Spending the day surfing or sunbathing on the sands where tourism in Bali began.*

○ **Legian Beach (p37)** *Savouring the legendary sunsets on this slightly calmer stretch of sea.*

○ **Double Six Beach (p40)** *Getting active with a pick-up game of beach volleyball or football with local revellers.*

○ **Bali Sea Turtle Society (p40)** *Re-releasing baby sea turtles at this responsible and respectable hatchery.*

Getting There & Around

🚌 Perama is the main tourist shuttle-bus operation in town. Kuta is a hub for the highly useful Kura-Kura tourist bus service. For public buses, you'll have to go to Denpasar first.

🚗 In traffic, a ride into Seminyak can top 150,000Rp and take more than 30 minutes; walking the beach will be quicker.

Kuta & Legian Map on p38

Top Experience 📷

Soak up the Sun on Kuta & Legian Beaches

It's the beach that put Kuta on the map. The strand of sand stretching for more than 12km from Tuban north to Kuta, Legian and beyond to Seminyak and Echo Beach is always a scene of surfing, massaging, games, chilling, imbibing and more. Sunsets are a time of gathering for just about everyone in south Bali. When conditions are right, you can enjoy an iridescent magenta spectacle: better than fireworks.

Kuta Beach

Tourism in Bali began on **Kuta Beach** (Map p38, C6; pictured) and is there any question why? Low-key hawkers will sell you soft drinks and beer, snacks and other treats, and you can rent surfboards, lounge chairs and umbrellas (negotiable at 10,000Rp to 20,000Rp), or just crash on the sand. The sunsets are legendary.

From Kuta, you can easily go surfing, sailing, diving or rafting anywhere in the southern part of Bali, or spend the day at a spa or amusement park, and still be back for the start of happy hour at sunset.

Surfing

The beach break called Halfway Kuta, offshore near the Hotel Istana Rama, is popular with novices. More challenging breaks can be found on the shifting sandbars off Legian, around the end of Jl Padma, and at Kuta Reef, 1km out to sea off Kuta Reef Beach.

Surf culture is huge in Kuta. Shops large and small sell megabrand surf gear and boards. Stalls on the side streets hire out surfboards (for a negotiable 50,000Rp per day) and bodyboards. They also repair dings and sell new and used boards. Some can arrange transport to nearby surfing spots. Used boards in good shape average US$200.

Legian Beach

An extension north from Kuta Beach, **Legian Beach** (Map p38, B3) is quieter thanks to the lack of a raucous road next to the sand, and fewer people. The area sprang up as an alternative to Kuta in the mid-1970s. At first it was a totally separate development, but these days you can't tell where one ends and the other begins.

★ Top Tips

o Take note of red flags on the beach. Even though swimming is typically safe along this stretch of sand, water conditions can change suddenly and rip tides and undertows are common here. When you see the flags, do not attempt to swim.

o If surfing, beware of strong waves, unpredictable currents and exposed rocks in the shallows. Chat with other surfers to assess the conditions beforehand.

✗ Take a Break

o Batu Bolong's a great place for a sunset – take in the view with the surfer crowd at Old Man's (p68).

Kuta & Legian

Jl Raya Kuta (Jl Imam Bonjol)

Jl Sunset

Jl Nakula

Jl Sunset

Jl Dewi Sri

Jl Dewi Sri

24

Sungai Mati

Jl Patih Jelantik

12

Jl Nakula

Jl Pura Puseh

Jl Nakula

20

Jl Legian

Gang Abdi

LEGIAN

Jl Raya Seminyak

Jl Arjuna (Jl Double Six)

Jl Pura Bagus Taruna
(Jl Werkudara)

Jl Padma Utara

Jl Padma (Jl Yudistra)

Jl Sahadewa

Jl Melasti

8 *Jamu*
Traditional Spa

27

10

11

Rip Curl
School
of Surf

7

Jl Pantai Kuta (Kuta Beach Rd)

Gate

Jl Pantai
Arjuna

Legian
Beach

Double Six
Beach **2**

19

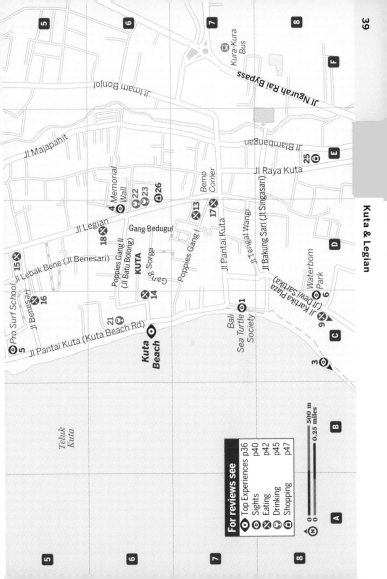

Kuta & Legian

Teluk
Kuta

Jl Ngurah Rai Bypass

Kura-Kura
Bus

Jl Imam Bonjol

Jl Majapahit

Jl Blambangan

25

Jl Raya Kuta

4 Memorial
Wall

22

23

26

Bemo
Corner

18

Jl Legian

Gang Bedugul

KUTA

15

Jl Lebak Bene (Jl Benesari)

Poppies Gang II
(Jl Batu Bolong)

13

17

16

Jl Benesari

Gang Sorga

Poppies Gang I

Jl Pantai Kuta

Jl Tengal Wangi

Jl Bakung Sari (Jl Singasari)

Pro Surf School

14

Waterbom
Park

6

5

21

Jl Kartika Plaza
(Jl Dewi Sartika)

9

Jl Pantai Kuta (Kuta Beach Rd)

Kuta
Beach

Bali
Sea Turtle
Society

1

3

For reviews see

◉	Top Experiences	p36
◎	Sights	p40
✪	Eating	p42
🅓	Drinking	p45
🅐	Shopping	p47

500 m
0.25 miles

N

Sights

Bali Sea Turtle Society

HATCHERY

1 ◎ MAP P38, C7

Bali Sea Turtle Society is a conservation group working to protect olive ridley turtles. It is one of the more responsible turtle hatcheries in Bali, re-releasing turtle hatchlings into the ocean from Kuta Beach around 4.30pm from April to October. Join the queue to collect your baby turtle in a small plastic water bath, pay a small donation, and join the group to release them. Signs offer excellent background info. Stop by an hour before the release time to ensure the activity is on for the day. (📞0811-388 2683; www.baliseaturtle.org; ⊗site 24hr, turtle releases 4.30pm Apr-Oct)

Double Six Beach

BEACH

2 ◎ MAP P38, A1

The beach becomes less crowded as you go north from Legian until very popular Double Six Beach, which is alive with pick-up games of football and volleyball all day long. It's a good place to meet partying locals. Watch out for water pollution after heavy rains.

Pantai Patra Jasa

BEACH

3 ◎ MAP P38, C8

This hidden gem is reached by a tiny access road along the fence on the north side of the airport. There's shade, a couple of tiny warungs (food stalls), views of planes landing and rarely ever a crowd. You can head north on the lovely beach walk to Kuta Beach.

Waterbom Park

EVGENY DRABLENKOV / SHUTTERSTOCK ©

Getting Away From it All

Dodging cars, motorcycles, touts, dogs and dodgy footpaths can make walking through this neighbourhood seem like anything but a holiday. You will soon be longing for uncrowded places where you hear little more than the rustling of palm fronds and the call of birds. Think you need a trip out of town? Well, think again. You can escape to the country without leaving the area. Swaths of undeveloped land and residential areas often hide behind the commercial strips.

In Legian, take any of the narrow *gang* (alleys) into the area bounded by Jl Legian, Jl Padma, Jl Padma Utara and Jl Pura Bagus Taruna and soon you'll be on narrow paths that go past local houses and the occasional simple warung or shop. Wander at random and enjoy the silence accented by, yes, the sound of palm fronds and birds.

Memorial Wall   MONUMENT

4 ⊙ MAP P38, D6

This memorial wall reflects the international scope of the 2002 bombings, and people from many countries pay their respects. Listing the names of the 202 known victims, including 88 Australians and 35 Indonesians, it is starting to look quite weathered. Across the street, a parking lot is all that is left of the destroyed Sari Club, site of the bombing. (Jl Legian)

Pro Surf School   SURFING

5 ⊙ MAP P38, C5

Right along Kuta Beach, this well-regarded school has been getting beginners standing for years. It offers all levels of lessons, including semi-private ones, plus gear and board rental. There are dorm rooms (from 150,000Rp), a pool and a cool cafe. (📞0361-751200; www.

prosurfschool.com; Jl Pantai Kuta 32; lessons per day from 675,000Rp)

Waterbom Park   WATER PARK

6 ⊙ MAP P38, C8

This watery amusement park covers 3.8 hectares of landscaped tropical gardens. It has assorted water slides (a couple dozen in total, including the 'Climax'), swimming pools, a FlowRider surf machine and a 'lazy river' ride. Other indulgences include a food court, a bar and a spa. (📞0361-755676; www.waterbom-bali.com; Jl Kartika Plaza; adult/child 535,000/385,000Rp; ⊙9am-6pm)

Rip Curl School of Surf   SURFING

7 ⊙ MAP P38, B2

Usually universities sell shirts with their logos; here it's the other way round: the beachwear company

Temple Festivals

Temple festivals in Bali are quite amazing, and you'll come across them unexpectedly, even in the most remote corners of the island. Each of the thousands of temples on the island has a 'temple birthday' known as an *odalan*. These are celebrated once every Balinese year of 210 days or every 354 to 356 days on the *saka* calendar (one of the two Balinese calendars).

Odalan are a very big deal and even the loneliest temple will spring to life around these special days. People from villages travel far to attend, and business owners in south Bali automatically give employees time off.

All night long there's activity, music and dancing – it's like a country fair, with food, amusements, gambling, colour and confusion. Finally, as dawn approaches, the entertainment fades away, the *pemangku* (temple priests) suggest to the gods that it's time they made their way back to heaven and the people wind their weary way back home.

Ask any locals you meet about current *odalan* or temple festivals. Seeing one may well be a highlight of your trip, particularly if it's at a major temple. Foreigners are welcome to watch the festivities and take photographs, but you should be unobtrusive and dress modestly.

sponsors a school. Lessons at all levels are given across the south; there are special courses for kids. It has a location for kitesurfing, windsurfing, diving, wakeboarding and stand-up paddle boarding (SUP) in Sanur. (📞0361-735858; www.ripcurlschoolofsurf.com; Jl Arjuna; lessons from 700,000Rp)

Jamu Traditional Spa   SPA

8 ◉ MAP P38, C4

In serene surrounds at a resort hotel you can enjoy a massage in rooms that open onto a pretty garden courtyard. If you've ever wanted to be part of a fruit cocktail, here's your chance – treatments involve tropical nuts, coconuts, papayas and more, often in fragrant baths. (📞0361-752520, ext 165; www.jamutraditionalspa.com; Jl Pantai Kuta, Alam Kul Kul; 1hr massage from 350,000Rp; ⊙9am-7pm)

Eating

Pisgor   INDONESIAN $

9 ✖ MAP P38, C8

All sorts of goodness emerges from the ever-bubbling deep-fryers at this narrow storefront near the airport. The *pisang goreng* (banana fritters) are not to be missed and you can enjoy more esoteric fare such as *ote-ote* (vegetable cakes). Get a mixed bag and munch away with raw chillies for accent. (Jl Dewi Sartika; treats from 2000Rp; ⏰10am-10pm)

Warung Murah INDONESIAN $

10 ❌ MAP P38, B1

Lunch goes swimmingly at this authentic warung specialising in seafood. An array of grilled fish awaits; if you prefer fowl over fin, the *sate ayam* is succulent *and* a bargain. Hugely popular at lunch; try to arrive right before noon. (☎0361-732082; Jl Arjuna; mains 20,000-35,000Rp; ⏰8am-11pm)

Warung Asia ASIAN $

11 ❌ MAP P38, B1

Staffed by waiters cheery even by Bali standards, this popular upstairs warung serves both Indo classics and Thai fare. It gets boozy and raucous at night. (www.warungasia.com; Jl Werkudara 5; mains from 50,000Rp; ⏰1.30-10.30pm; 📶)

Take JAPANESE $$

12 ❌ MAP P38, D4

Flee Bali for a relaxed version of Tokyo just by ducking under the traditional curtain over the doorway at this ever-expanding restaurant. Hyper-fresh sushi, sashimi and more are prepared under the keen eyes of a team of chefs behind a long counter. The head chef is a stalwart at the Jimbaran fish market in the early hours. (☎0361-759745; www.take.ramarestaurantsbali.com; Jl Patih Jelantik; mains 70,000-300,000Rp; ⏰11am-midnight; 📶)

Kuta & Legian Eating

Sunset drinks on Kuta Beach (p45)

ASIATRAVEL / SHUTTERSTOCK©

Poppies Restaurant

INDONESIAN $$

13 MAP P38, D7

Opening its doors in 1973, Poppies was one of the first restaurants established in Kuta (Poppies Gang I is even named after it). It's popular for its elegant garden setting and a menu of upmarket Balinese, Western and Thai cuisine. The *rijstaffel* (selection of dishes served with rice) and seafood is popular. (0361-751059; www.poppiesbali.com; Poppies Gang I; mains 50,000-135,000Rp; 8am-11pm;)

Fat Chow

ASIAN $$

14 MAP P38, C6

A stylish, modern take on the traditional open-fronted cafe, Fat Chow serves Asian-accented fare at long picnic tables, small tables and lounges. The food is creative, with dishes for sharing. Among the favourites: crunchy Asian salad, pork buns, Tokyo prawns and authentic pad Thai. (0361-753516; www.fatchowbali.com; Poppies Gang II; mains from 65,000Rp; 9am-11pm;)

Mama's German Restaurant

GERMAN $$

15 MAP P38, D5

Once you get used to the local serving staff in full German dirndl, you might almost think you're in a sweatier version of Munich. The menu is authentic German, with a vast selection of sausages, roasts and pork steaks from the restaurant's own private butcher. (Nonwurst choices include burgers,

Women in traditional clothing during a festival

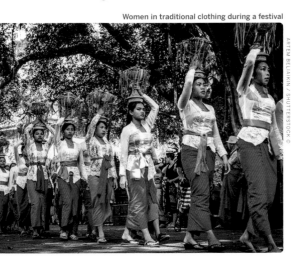

ARTEM BELIAIKIN / SHUTTERSTOCK ©

Sunset Drinks on Kuta & Legian

Bali sunsets regularly explode in stunning displays of reds, oranges and purples. Sipping a cold one while watching this free show to the beat of the surf is the top activity at 6pm. Genial local guys offer plastic chairs on the sand and cheap, cold Bintang (20,000Rp).

In Kuta, head to the car-free south end of the beach; in Legian, the best place is the strip of beach that starts north of Jl Padma and runs to the south end of Jl Pantai Arjuna.

noodles, pizza etc.) Quaff draught Bintang by the litre. (☏0361-761151; www.bali-mamas.com; Jl Legian; mains from 65,000Rp; ⏲24hr)

Balcony   INTERNATIONAL $$

16 ✕ MAP P38, C5

The Balcony has a breezy tropical design and sits above the din of Jl Benesari below. Get ready for the day with something from the long breakfast menu. At night choose from pasta, grilled meats and a few Indo classics. It's all nicely done and the perfect place for an impromptu date night. (☏0361-757409; www.thebalconybali.com; Jl Benesari 16; mains 50,000-170,000Rp; ⏲6am-11pm)

Made's Warung   INDONESIAN $$

17 ✕ MAP P38, D7

Made's was the original tourist warung in Kuta and its Westernised Indonesian menu has been much copied. Classic dishes such as *nasi campur* (rice with a choice of side dishes) are served in an open-fronted setting that harks back to when Kuta's tourist hot spots were

lit by gas lantern. (☏0361-732130; www.madeswarung.com; Jl Pantai Kuta; mains from 60,000Rp; ⏲8am-11pm)

Kopi Pot   CAFE $$

18 ✕ MAP P38, D6

Shaded by trees, Kopi Pot is a favourite, popular for its coffees, milkshakes and myriad desserts. The multilevel, open-air dining area and bar sits back from noxious Jl Legian. (☏0361-752614; www.kopipot.com; Jl Legian; mains from 43,000Rp; ⏲7am-11pm; 📶)

Drinking

Double-Six Rooftop   BAR

19 🍸 MAP P38, A1

Sharks in aquarium-lined walls, suave lounges and tiki torches: this ostentatious bar above the Double-Six hotel could be the lair of a Bond villain. Amazing sunset views are best enjoyed from the circular booths – a minimum 1,000,000Rp spend to reserve one is redeemable against food, and perfect for groups. Drinks are pricey. (☏0361-734300; www.doublesixrooftop.com; Double Six Beach 66; ⏲3-11pm; 📶)

Follow the Party

Bali's most infamous clubs cluster in about a 300m radius of Sky Garden Lounge. The distinction between drinking and clubbing is blurry at best, with one morphing into another as the night wears on (or the morning comes up). Most bars are free to enter, and often have special drink promotions and 'happy hours' that run at various intervals until after midnight. Savvy partygoers follow the specials from venue to venue and enjoy a massively discounted night out. Look for cut-price-drinks coupon fliers.

Bali club ambience ranges from the laid-back vibe of the surfer dives to high-concept nightclubs with long drink menus and hordes of prowling servers. Prostitutes have proliferated at some Kuta clubs.

Jenja   CLUB

20 MAP P38, C1

A very slick, high-concept nightclub in the TS Suites hotel, spread over several levels. DJs rev it up with disco, R&B, funk, soul and techno. The crowd is a mix of well-heeled locals and expats. The restaurant serves upmarket fare that is good for sharing. (0361-882 7711; www.clubjenja.com; TS Suites, Jl Nakula 18; 10pm-4am Wed & Thu, to 5am Fri & Sat)

Velvet   BAR

21 MAP P38, C6

The sunset views can't be beat at this large terrace bar and cafe at the beach end of the Beachwalk mall. It morphs into a club after 10pm Wednesday to Sunday. Grab a lounger for two. (0361-846 4928; Jl Pantai Kuta, Beachwalk, level 3; 11am-late)

Sky Garden Lounge   CLUB

22 MAP P38, D6

This multilevel palace of flash flirts with height restrictions from its rooftop bar where all of Kuta twinkles around you. Look for top DJs, a ground-level cafe and paparazzi-wannabes. Possibly Kuta's most iconic club, with hourly drink specials and a buffet. Gets backpackers, drunken teens, locals on the make etc. (www.skygarden bali.com; Jl Legian 61; from 99,000Rp; 5pm-4am)

Bounty   CLUB

23 MAP P38, D6

Set on a faux sailing boat amid a mini-mall of food and drink, the Bounty is a vast open-air disco that pumps all night to hip-hop, techno, house and party tracks. Foam parties, go-go dancers, drag shows and cheap shots add to the rowdiness. (Jl Legian; 10pm-3am)

Shopping

Luke Studer   SPORTS & OUTDOORS

24 🔒 MAP P38, E3

Legendary board-shaper Luke Studer works from this large and glossy shop. Short boards, retro fishes, single fins and classic longboards are sold ready-made or custom-built. (📞0361-894 7425; www.studersurfboards.com; Jl Dewi Sri 7A; ⏱9am-8pm)

Joger   GIFTS & SOUVENIRS

25 🔒 MAP P38, E8

This Bali retail legend is the most popular store in the south. Mobs come for doe-eyed plastic puppies or one of thousands of T-shirts bearing wry, funny or simply inexplicable phrases (almost all are limited edition). In fact, the sign out front says 'Pabrik Kata-Kata', which

means 'factory of words'. Warning: conditions inside the cramped store are insane. (📞0361-752523; www.jogerjelek.com; Jl Raya Kuta; ⏱10am-8pm)

Surfer Girl   CLOTHING

26 🔒 MAP P38, E6

A local legend, this vast store for girls of all ages has a winsome logo that says it all. Clothes, gear, bikinis and plenty of other stuff in every shade of bubblegum ever made is available. (📞0361-752693; www.surfer-girl.com; Jl Legian 138; ⏱9.30am-11pm)

Sriwijaya Batik   TEXTILES

27 🔒 MAP P38, B1

Makes batik and other fabrics to order in infinite colours. Great browsing. (📞0878-6150 0510; Jl Arjuna 19; ⏱9am-6pm)

Explore ⊕
Seminyak

Dynamic Seminyak is home to scores of restaurants and clubs and a wealth of creative, designer shops and galleries. World-class hotels line the beach, and what a beach it is – as wide and sandy as Kuta's but slightly less crowded. With its intangible sense of style, Seminyak feels almost like it's on another island. You could easily spend your entire holiday here.

The Short List

○ **Seminyak Beach (p52)** *Enjoying an ice-cold cocktail with sunset views.*

○ **La Favela (p55)** *Dancing your way from room to room in this themed nightlife hot spot.*

○ **BIASA ArtSpace (p52)** *Imbibing the works of Indonesia's up-and-coming artists.*

○ **Pura Petitenget (p52)** *Taking in an anniversary celebration at this important seaside temple.*

Getting There & Around

🚌 The Kura-Kura tourist bus has a route linking Seminyak with Umalas in the north and Kuta in the south; however, it runs infrequently.

🚕 Metered taxis are easily hailed. A trip from the airport with the airport taxi cartel costs about 250,000Rp. Blue Bird has the most reliable taxi service.

Seminyak Map on p50

Seminyak beachside bar GABI LUKA / SHUTTERSTOCK ©

Seminyak

A B C D

1

Kerobokan
Beach

Jl Petitenget

Pura
Petitenget **3**

Jl Pura Telaga Waja

10

Jl Kayu Jati

Jl Braban

Jl Pangkung Sari

28
23 **20** **12**

7

Seminyak
Beach **1**

Jl Kayu Aya

19

16

2

Jl Petitenget

Jl Kayu Aya

3

Teluk
Kuta

Jl Sarinande

4

Jl Sarinande

5

For reviews see

◉	Sights	p52
✖	Eating	p53
🍷	Drinking	p55
🔒	Shopping	p57

N 0 ———————————— 500 m
   0 ———————————— 0.25 miles

17

6

A B C D

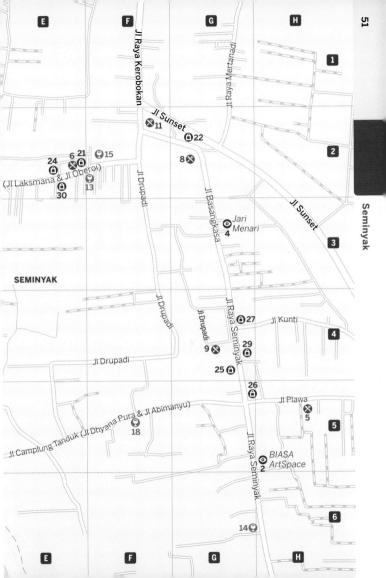

E   F   G   H

Seminyak

1

2

3

4

5

6

Jl Raya Kerobokan

Jl Raya Mertanadi

Jl Sunset
⊗11

🔒22

Jl Sunset

24
🔒
6 21
🔒
⊗🔒
🚍15

8⊗

Jl Drupadi

(Jl Laksmana & Jl Oberoi)

🚍13

🔒
30

Jl Basangkasa

◉ Jari
Menari
4

SEMINYAK

Jl Drupadi

Jl Drupadi

Jl Drupadi

Jl Raya Seminyak

🔒27   Jl Kunti

29
🔒

9⊗

25 🔒

26
🔒

Jl Plawa

⊗
5

Jl Camplung Tanduk (Jl Dhyana Pura & Jl Abimanyu)

18

Jl Raya Seminyak

◉ BIASA
ArtSpace
2

14🚍

E   F   G   H

Sights

Seminyak Beach
BEACH

1 ⊙ MAP P50, A2

A sunset lounger and an ice-cold Bintang on the beach at sunset is simply magical. A good stretch can be found near Pura Petitenget, and it tends to be less crowded than further south in Kuta.

BIASA ArtSpace
GALLERY

2 ⊙ MAP P50, H5

Founded in 2005, BIASA ArtSpace showcases the work of up-and-coming Indonesian and international artists. The gallery has a line-up of rotating exhibitions in a variety of art forms, from painting and photography to sculpture and installation art. The upper floor houses a mini library and a restoration studio. (☏0361-730308; www.biasagroup.com; Jl Raya Seminyak 34; admission free; ⊘9am-9pm)

Pura Petitenget
HINDU TEMPLE

3 ⊙ MAP P50, B2

Pura Petitenget is an important temple and the scene of many ceremonies. It is one of a string of sea temples that stretches from Pura Luhur Ulu Watu on the Bukit peninsula north to Pura Tanah Lot in western Bali. Petitenget loosely translates as 'magic box'; it was a treasured belonging of the legendary 16th-century priest Nirartha, who refined the Balinese religion and visited this site often.

Seminyak Beach

JOKOLEO / GETTY IMAGES ©

The temple is renowned for its anniversary celebrations on the Balinese 210-day calendar. It is right next to Pura Masceti. (Jl Petitenget)

Jari Menari
SPA

4 ⊙ MAP P50, G3

Jari Menari is true to its name, which means 'dancing fingers': your body will be one happy dance floor. The all-male staff use massage techniques that emphasise rhythm. It also offers classes in giving massage (from US$170). (☎0361-736740; www.jarimenari.com; Jl Raya Basangkasa 47; sessions from 435,000Rp; ⊙9am-9pm)

Eating

Warung Taman Bambu
BALINESE $

5 ✖ MAP P50, H5

This classic warung may look simple from the street but the comfy tables are – like the many fresh and spicy dishes on offer – a cut above the norm. There's a small stand for *babi guling* (spit-roast pig) right next door. (☎0361-888 1567; Jl Plawa 10; mains from 28,000Rp; ⊙10am-10pm; 🛜)

Warung Aneka Rasa
INDONESIAN $

6 ✖ MAP P50, E2

Keeping things real in the heart of Seminyak's upmarket retail strip, this humble warung cooks up Indo classics in an inviting

Finding Your Inner Goddess

Surf Goddess (☎0858 997 0808; www.surfgoddessretreats. com; per week incl private room from US$2495) organises surf holidays for women that include lessons, yoga, meals and accommodation in a posh guesthouse in the backstreets of Seminyak.

open-front cafe. It's a refuge from the buzz. (☎0812 361 7937; Jl Kayu Aya; mains from 25,000Rp; ⊙7am-7pm)

Bali Bakery
CAFE $

7 ✖ MAP P50, C2

The best feature of the Seminyak Sq open-air mall is this bakery with its shady tables and long menu of baked goods, salads, sandwiches and other fine fare. It's a good place to linger before heading back out to shop. (☎0361-738033; www.balibakery.com; Jl Kayu Aya, Seminyak Sq; mains 40,000-70,000Rp; ⊙7.30am-10.30pm; 🛜)

Warung Ibu Made
INDONESIAN $

8 ✖ MAP P50, G2

The woks roar almost from dawn to dusk amid the constant hubbub on this busy corner of Jl Raya Seminyak, where several stalls cook food fresh under the shade of a huge banyan tree. Refresh yourself with the juice

Seminyak's Curving Spine 💬

The thriving heart of Seminyak is along meandering Jl Kayu Aya (aka Jl Oberoi/Jl Laksmana). It heads towards the beach from bustling Jl Basangkasa and then turns north through a part of Seminyak along Jl Petitenget. The road is lined with a profusion of restaurants, upmarket boutiques and hotels as it winds through Seminyak and into Kerobokan. Pavements have hugely improved their window-shopping and cafe-hopping offerings; now it's the drivers stuck in traffic who fume.

of a young coconut. (Jl Basangkasa; mains from 15,000Rp; ⊙7am-7pm)

Shelter Cafe AUSTRALIAN $$

9 🍴 MAP P50, G4

This second-storey cafe brims daily with the young, beautiful people of Seminyak, their coffee strong, their acai bowls piled high (those are actually from Nalu Bowls, the acai bar downstairs). With an extensive menu of healthy fare, it's the top brunch spot in Seminyak, and a cultural hub and host of things like pop-up fashion stores and parties on weekends. (📞0813 3770 6471; www.sheltercafebali.com; Jl Drupadi; mains 55,000-95,000Rp; ⊙8am-6pm; 📶)

Nalu Bowls HEALTH FOOD $$

Inspired by Hawaii's culture and tropical ingredients, this chain of acai bowl establishments has made a big splash in Bali. The flagship Seminyak restaurant occupies just a small bar downstairs from Shelter Cafe (see 9 🍴 Map p50, G4), but the line sometimes extends down the block for the fresh fruit and smoothie bowls topped with homemade granola and bananas. (📞0812 3660 9776; www.nalubowls.com; Jl Drupadi; 60,000-80,000Rp; ⊙7.30am-6pm)

Motel Mexicola MEXICAN $$

10 🍴 MAP P50, B2

Not your average taqueria, Motel Mexicola is an extravaganza that channels a tropical version of a nightclub. The huge space is decked out in kitschy neon and palm trees. Food is secondary to drinks: soft corn tortilla tacos filled with tempura prawn or shredded pork, along with meaty mains.

Cocktails, served in copper kettles, are a treat on a balmy evening. (📞0361-736688; www.motelmexicolabali.com; Jl Kayu Jati 9; mains from 60,000Rp; ⊙11am-1am)

Mama San FUSION $$

11 🍴 MAP P50, F2

One of Seminyak's most popular restaurants, this stylish warehouse-sized space is split into levels, with photographs hanging from exposed brick walls. The menu has an emphasis on creative dishes from across Southeast Asia. A long cocktail list provides liquid balm for the mojito set and has lots of tropical-flavoured pours. (📞0361-730436; www.mamasanbali.com; Jl Raya Kerobokan 135; mains 90,000-200,000Rp; 🕐noon-3pm & 6.30-11pm; ❄️📶)

Sisterfields

CAFE $$

12 ⊗ MAP P50, D2

Trendy Sisterfields does classic Aussie breakfasts such as smashed avocado, and more-inventive dishes such as salmon Benedict and maple-roasted-pumpkin salad. There are also hipster faves such as pulled-pork rolls and shakshuka poached eggs. Grab a seat at a booth, at the counter or in the rear courtyard. There are several other good coffee cafes nearby. (📞0361-738454; www.sisterfieldsbali.com; Jl Kayu Cendana 7; mains 85,000-140,000Rp; 🕐7am-10pm; 📶)

Drinking

La Favela

BAR

13 🍺 MAP P50, F2

An alluring, mysterious entry seduces you into full bohemian flair at La Favela, one of Bali's coolest and most original nightspots. Themed rooms lead you on a confounding tour from dimly lit speakeasy cocktail lounges and antique dining rooms to graffiti-splashed bars. Tables are cleared after 11pm to make way for DJs and a dance floor.

It's equally popular for its garden restaurant, which has a Mediterranean-inspired menu.

Seminyak Drinking

Mama San

(☎0812-4612 0010; www.lafavela.com; Jl Kayu Aya 177X; ⏰5pm-late; 📶)

Ryoshi Seminyak
House of Jazz
BAR

14 🚇 MAP P50, G6

The Seminyak branch of the Bali chain of Japanese restaurants has live jazz three nights a week on an intimate stage under a traditionally thatched roof. Expect some of the best local and visiting talent. (☎0361-731152; www.ryoshibali.com; Jl Raya Seminyak 17; ⏰noon-midnight, music from 9pm Mon, Wed & Fri)

Red Carpet
Champagne Bar
BAR

15 🚇 MAP P50, F2

Choose from more than 200 types of champagne at this over-the-top glam bar on Seminyak's couture strip. Waltz the red carpet and toss back a few namesake flutes while contemplating a raw oyster and displays of frilly frocks. It's open to the street (but elevated, darling) so you can gaze down on the masses. (☎0361-737889; www.redcarpetchampagnebar.com; Jl Kayu Aya 42; ⏰1pm-4am)

Revolver
CAFE

16 🚇 MAP P50, D3

Wander down a tiny *gang* and push through narrow wooden doors to reach this matchbox coffee bar that does an excellent selection of brews. There are just a few tables in the creatively retro room that's styled like a Wild West saloon; nab one and enjoy tasty fresh bites for breakfast and lunch. (☎0851 0088

La Plancha

4968; www.revolverespresso.com; off Jl Kayu Aya; coffee 28,000-55,000Rp, mains from 55,000Rp; 🕙7am-mid-night; 🛜)

La Plancha
BAR

17 🚇 MAP P50, D6

The most substantial of the beach bars along the beach walk south of Jl Camplung Tanduk, La Plancha has its share of ubiquitous brightly coloured umbrellas and beanbags on the sand, plus a typical beach menu (pizzas, noodles etc). After sunset, expect DJs and beach parties. (📞0878 6141 6310; www.laplancha-bali.com; off Jl Camplung Tanduk; 🕙9am-11pm)

Bali Joe
GAY & LESBIAN

18 🚇 MAP P50, F5

One of several lively LGBTIQ+ venues along this strip. Drag queens and go-go dancers rock the house nightly. (📞0361-300 3499; www.balijoebar.com; Jl Camplung Tanduk; 🕙4pm-3am; 🛜)

Shopping

Drifter Surf Shop
FASHION & ACCESSORIES

19 🔒 MAP P50, D2

High-end surf fashion, surfboards, gear, cool books and brands such as Obey and Wegener. Started by two savvy surfer dudes, the shop stocks goods noted for their individuality and high quality. (📞0361-733274; www.driftersurf.com; Jl Kayu Aya 50; 🕙9am-11pm)

Seminyak Sunsets

At the beach end of Jl Camplung Tanduk you have a choice: turn left for a beachy frolic at the string of beach bars, both simple and plush; or turn right for trendy beach clubs like Ku De Ta, or cheery vendors offering cheap Bintang, a plastic chair and maybe some amateur guitar music.

Seminyak Village
MALL

20 🔒 MAP P50, C2

Rice fields just a few years ago, this air-con mall deserves a compliment for being discreetly placed back from the street. The selection of shops is refreshingly local, with some notable names, such as Lily Jean (p58), on the three levels. The small carts leased to up-and-coming Balinese designers is a nice touch. (📞0361-738097; www.seminyakvillage.com; Jl Kayu Jati 8; 🕙9am-10pm; 🛜)

Thaikila
CLOTHING

21 🔒 MAP P50, E2

'The dream bikini of all women' is the motto of this local brand that makes a big statement with its tiny wear. The swimwear is French-designed and made right in Bali. If you need something stylish for the beach, come here. (📞0361-731130; www.thaikila.com; Jl Kayu Aya; 🕙9am-9pm)

Shopping in Seminyak

Seminyak has it all: designer boutiques (Bali has a thriving fashion industry), retro-chic stores, slick galleries, wholesale emporiums and family-run workshops.

The best shopping starts on Jl Raya Seminyak at Bintang Supermarket and runs north through Jl Basangkasa. The retail strip branches off into Jl Kayu Aya and Jl Kayu Jati while continuing north on Jl Raya Kerobokan into Kerobokan. Avoid stepping into a yawning pavement cavern.

Souq
HOMEWARES

22 🔒 MAP P50, G2

The Middle East meets Asia at this glossy high-concept store with Bali-designed housewares and clothing. It has a small cafe with healthy breakfast and lunch choices plus good coffee and cold-pressed juices. (📞 0822 3780 1817; www.souqstore.co; Jl Basangkasa 10; ⏰ 8am-8pm)

Kody & Ko
ART

23 🔒 MAP P50, C2

The polychromatic critters in the window set the tone for this vibrant shop of art and decorator items. There's a large attached gallery with regular exhibitions. (📞 0361-737359; www.kodyandko.com; Jl Kayu Jati 4A; ⏰ 9am-9pm)

Uma & Leopold
CLOTHING

24 🔒 MAP P50, E2

Luxe clothes and little frilly things to put on before slipping off... Designed in Bali by a French couple. (📞 0361-737697; www.umaandleopold. com; Jl Kayu Aya 77X; ⏰ 9am-9pm)

Lily Jean
CLOTHING

Selling mostly Bali-made items, this designer shop in Seminyak Village (see 20 🔒 Map p50, C2) combines international allure with local motifs. (📞 0811 398 272; www. lily-jean.com; Jl Kayu Jati 8, Seminyak Village, 1st fl; ⏰ 9am-10pm)

Theatre Art Gallery
ARTS & CRAFTS

25 🔒 MAP P50, G4

Specialises in vintage and reproduction *wayang* puppets used in traditional Balinese theatre. Just looking at the animated faces peering back at you is a delight. (📞 0361-732782; Jl Raya Seminyak; ⏰ 9am-8pm)

Domicil
HOMEWARES

26 🔒 MAP P50, G5

Facade meets merchandise: everything is designed with colonial flair at this appealing housewares shop. (📞 0818 0569 8417; www. domicil-living.com; Jl Raya Seminyak 56; ⏰ 10am-10pm)

Ashitaba
ARTS & CRAFTS

27 🔒 MAP P50, G4

Tenganan, the Aga village of east Bali, produces the intricate and beautiful rattan items sold here. Containers, bowls, purses and more (from 50,000Rp) all display the very fine weaving. (📞0361-737054; Jl Raya Seminyak 6; ⏰9am-9pm)

White Peacock
HOMEWARES

28 🔒 MAP P50, C2

Styled like a country cottage, this is the place for cute cushions, throw rugs, table linens and more. (📞0361-733238; Jl Kayu Jati 1; ⏰9am-8pm)

Indivie
ARTS & CRAFTS

29 🔒 MAP P50, G4

The works of young designers based in Bali are showcased at this intriguing and glossy boutique. (📞0361-730927; www.indivie.com; Jl Raya Seminyak, Made's Warung; ⏰10am-11pm)

Bamboo Blonde
CLOTHING

30 🔒 MAP P50, E2

Shop for frilly, sporty or sexy frocks and formal wear at this cheery designer boutique (one of 11 island-wide). All goods are designed and made in Bali. (📞0361-731864; www.bambooblonde.com; Jl Kayu Aya 61; ⏰10am-10pm)

Explore ◈
Kerobokan
& Canggu

Continuing seamlessly north from Seminyak, Kerobokan combines some of Bali's best restaurants and shopping, lavish lifestyles and still more beach. More a state of mind than a place, Canggu is the catch-all name given to the villa-filled stretch of land between Kerobokan and Echo Beach. It's packed with an ever-more alluring collection of businesses, especially casual cafes.

The Short List

○ **Batu Bolong Beach (p65)** Mingling with a mix of locals, expats and visitors hanging out in the cafes.

○ **Echo Beach (p65)** Catching waves at one of Bali's most popular surf breaks.

○ **Beach Clubs (p68)** Imbibing cocktails and sunshine at creative, chilled-out watering holes.

Getting There & Around

🚗 You'll need your own wheels to get here, whether it's a car and driver or a motorbike.

🚕 The beach areas usually have a taxi monopoly that will charge upwards of 150,000Rp for a ride to Seminyak.

Kerobokan & Canggu Map on p64

Berawa Beach (p63), Canggu WESTEND61 / GETTY IMAGES ©

Walking Tour 🥾

Batubelig Beach to Pererenan Beach

This is a fascinating stroll where you'll see temples, fishing encampments, crashing surf, surfers, cool cafes and outcrops of upscale beach culture. The only catch is that after heavy rains some of the rivers may be too deep to cross, especially the one just northwest of Batubelig. Put your gear in waterproof bags in case you have to do some fording, and you can always find taxis at any of the larger beaches if needed.

Start Batubelig Beach
End Pererenan Beach
Length 4km; 1 to 2 hours

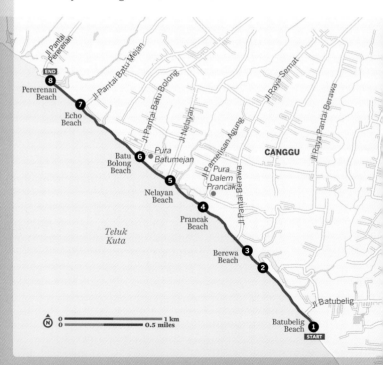

❶ Batubelig Beach

Reached via Jl Batubelig, the sand narrows here but there are some great spots for a drink, both grand and simple, and it's a good place to start a walk along the curving sands northwest. Look along the beach and you can see the developments at Echo Beach in the distance, as you begin an adventure that can take anywhere from an hour to half a day depending on your whim.

❷ Water Crossing

The biggest obstacle on this walk is about 500m from the start. The river and lagoon here flow into the ocean, often to a depth of 1m and after rains much deeper. If so, take the little footbridge over the lagoon and look for the groovy outdoor lounge La Laguna (which may have reopened after COVID-19).

❸ Berawa Beach

Now one of Canggu's hip centres, this stretch of beach has high-concept Finn's Recreation Club (p66) and is about 2km up the sand from Seminyak (where you can also begin this walk). There are also low-key beer vendors by the pounding sea. Look along the sand's edge for the vast Marabito Art Villa, a private estate that's an architectural wonder.

❹ Prancak Beach

Almost 1km further on you'll come to another (shallow) water crossing that also marks the large complex of **Pura Dalem Prancak** (Jl Pantai Prancak). Vendors offer drinks and surfboard rental on Pantai Prancak; turn around facing the way you've come and you can see the sweep of the beach all the way to the airport.

❺ Nelayan Beach

A collection of fishing boats and huts marks this mellow stretch of sand that lacks easy access to the raw energy of Canggu just inland.

❻ Batu Bolong Beach

Hip and popular Batu Bolong Beach is home to the large **Pura Batumejan** (Jl Pantai Batu Bolong) complex, with a striking pagoda-like temple. There are surfboard rentals, cafes – such as the legendary hang-out Old Man's (p68) – and a vibrant mix of people. Drink vendors service loungers on the sand.

❼ Echo Beach

At Echo Beach, reward yourself for your adventurous walk at the many cafes. A flock of shops means you can replace any clothes that are drenched beyond repair. Otherwise, take your camera out of its waterproof bag and nab shots of the popular surf break.

❽ Pererenan Beach

Just 300m west of Echo Beach is the region's next hot spot, Pererenan Beach, reached via sand and rock formations. You'll be spoiled by the dozen food and drink joints built right on the sand. But all that's needed is one developer to sneeze and they'll all be gone.

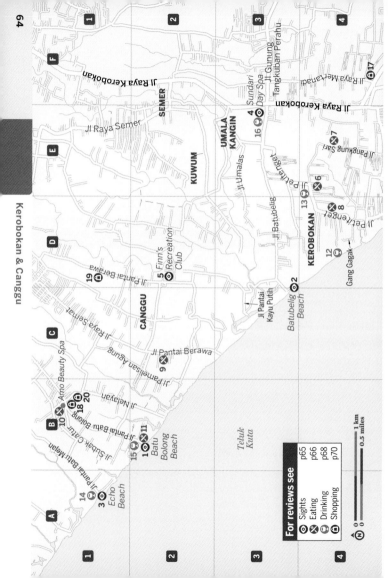

64

Kerobokan & Canggu

Jl Raya Kerobokan

F

SEMER

Jl Raya Semer

E

KUWUM

UMALA KANGIN

Sundari 4 Day Spa
16 ❌❶

Jl Gunung Tangkuban Perahu

Jl Raya Kerobokan

Jl Umalas

Jl Petitenget

3

❌ 7
Jl Pangkung Sari

Jl Raya Mekranadi

🏨 17 **4**

Jl Batubelig

❌ 6
Jl Pe...

KEROBOKAN

13 ❶

❌ 8
Jl Petitenget

12 🏨
Gang Gagak

D

Finn's 5
Recreation Club ◎

Jl Pantai Berawa
19 🏨

CANGGU

Jl Pantai Kayu Putih

Batubelig 2 ◎
Beach

C

Jl Raya Semat

Jl Pamelisan Agung

Jl Pantai Berawa
❌ 9

Jl Nelayan

Arno Beauty Spa

18 🏨 20

B

10 ❌
Jl Pantai Batu Bolong

15 ❶ 1 ❌❶ 11

Batu Bolong Beach

Jl Subak Catur

Teluk Kuta

A

Jl Pantai Batu Mejan

14 ❶
3 ❌

Echo Beach

For reviews see

◎ Sights	p65
❌ Eating	p66
❶ Drinking	p68
🏨 Shopping	p70

Ⓝ
0 _____ 1 km
0 _____ 0.5 miles

1

2

3

4

Sights

Batu Bolong Beach
BEACH

1  MAP P64, B2

The beach at Batu Bolong is the most popular in the Canggu area. There's almost always a good mix of locals, expats and visitors hanging out in the cafes, surfing the breaks or watching it all from the sand. There are rental loungers, umbrellas and beer vendors. (parking motorbike/car 2000/5000Rp)

Batubelig Beach
BEACH

2 MAP P64, D3

The sand narrows here but there are some good places for a drink, both grand and simple. Easily reached via Jl Batubelig, this is a likely place to start a walk along the curving sands northwest to popular beaches as far as Echo Beach. About 500m north, a river and lagoon flow into the ocean, sometimes up to 1m deep – after rains it may be much deeper. In this case, take the little footbridge over the lagoon and see if La Laguna has reopened, from where you can call a taxi.

Echo Beach
BEACH

3 MAP P64, A1

Surfers and those who like to watch them flock here for the high-tide left-hander that regularly tops 2m. The greyish sand right in front of the developments can vanish at high tide, but you'll find wide strands east and west. Batu Bolong Beach is 500m east. (Pantai Batu Mejan)

Kerobokan & Canggu Sights

Coastline near Echo Beach

DUDAREV MIKHAIL / SHUTTERSTOCK ©

Amo Beauty Spa

With some of Asia's top models lounging about, **Amo Beauty Spa** (Map p64, B1; ☎0361-907 1146; www.amospa.com; Jl Pantai Batu Bolong 69; massages from 230,000Rp; ⏱8am-10pm) feels like you've stumbled into a *Vogue* shoot. In addition to massages, services range from haircare to pedicures and unisex waxing. Book ahead.

Sundari Day Spa   SPA

4 ⊙ MAP P64, E3

This much-recommended spa strives to offer the services of a five-star resort without the high prices. The massage oils and other potions are organic, and there's a full menu of therapies and treatments on offer. (☎0361-735073; www.sundari-dayspa.com; Jl Petitenget 7; massages from 250,000Rp; ⏱10am-10pm)

Finn's Recreation Club   HEALTH & FITNESS

5 ⊙ MAP P64, D2

Bali's expats shuttlecock themselves silly at Finn's Recreation Club, a New Age version of something you'd expect to find during the Raj. The vast, perfectly virescent lawn is manicured for croquet. Get sweaty with tennis, squash, polo, cricket, bowling, the spa or the 25m pool. Many villa rentals include guest passes here. The garish **Splash Waterpark** is popular. (☎0361-848 3939; www.finnsrecclub.com; Jl Raya Pantai Berawa; adult/child day pass 450,000/300,000Rp; ⏱6am-9pm)

Eating

Warung Eny   BALINESE $

6 ✕ MAP P64, E4

The eponymous Eny cooks everything herself at this tiny open-front warung nearly hidden behind various potted plants. Look for the roadside sign that captures the vibe: 'The love cooking'. The seafood, such as large prawns smothered in garlic, is delicious and most ingredients are organic. Ask about Eny's excellent cooking classes. (☎0361-473 6892; warungeny@yahoo.com; Jl Petitenget 97; mains from 35,000Rp; ⏱8am-11pm)

Sangsaka   INDONESIAN $$

7 ✕ MAP P64, E4

On a Kerobokan backstreet, this casual restaurant serves well-nuanced versions of Indonesian dishes drawn from across the archipelago. Many are cooked over various types of charcoal, which vary depending on the origin of the dish. The dining area is done up in the usual vintage-wood motif, with just a touch more polish than usual. It has a good bar.

(☎0812 3695 9895; www.sangsaka-bali.com; Jl Pangkung Sari 100; mains 80,000-180,000Rp; ⏰6pm-midnight Tue-Sun)

Saigon Street VIETNAMESE $$

8 ✂ MAP P64, D4

Modern, vibrant and packed, this Vietnamese restaurant lures in the buzzing masses with its swanky neon decor. Creative Vietnamese dishes include peppery betel leaves filled with slow-cooked octopus, and there's an impressive rice-paper roll selection, along with curries, *pho* (rice-noodle soup) and grilled meats cooked on aromatic coconut wood. Cocktails include the 'bang bang' martini, a chilled bit of boozy splendour. Book ahead. (☎0361-897 4007; www.saigonstreetbali.com; Jl Petitenget 77; mains 50,000-175,000Rp; ⏰11am-1am; 🔊)

Creamery ICE CREAM $

9 ✂ MAP P64, C2

Learn the meaning of true small-batch ice cream at this cheery shop that churns its creations one serving at a time, employing liquid nitrogen for instant freezing. House-created sundaes are decadent in their simplicity – and you can build your own if you're feeling creative. Alternatively, enjoy an ice cream sandwich or milkshake for something a bit tamer. (☎0819 9982 5898; www.facebook.com/CreameryBali; Jl Pantai Berawa 8; sundaes from 35,000Rp; ⏰11.30am-10.30pm)

Echo Beach (p65)

SHEMYAKINA TATIANA/SHUTTERSTOCK ©

Drinks on Echo Beach

Enjoying a drink while watching the surf break is an Echo Beach tradition. Just west of the main cafe cluster is a string of ephemeral beach bars that are little more than bamboo shacks. Both atmospheric and relaxed, you'll find beanbags on the sand, and cold beer at hand.

Deus Ex Machina
CAFE $$

10 MAP P64, B1

This surreal venue amid Canggu's rice fields has many personas. If you're hungry, it's a restaurant-cafe-bar; for shoppers, it's a fashion label; if you're into culture, it's a contemporary-art gallery; for music lovers, it's a live-gig venue (Sunday afternoons) for local punk bands; for bikers, it's a custom-made motorcycle shop; if you want your beard trimmed, it's a barber... (Temple of Enthusiasm; ☑0811 388 150; www.deuscustoms.com; Jl Batu Mejan 8; mains 60,000-170,000Rp; ⏰7am-11pm; 🛜)

Old Man's
INTERNATIONAL $$

11 MAP P64, B2

You'll have a tough time deciding just where to sit to enjoy your drink at this popular coastal beer garden overlooking Batu Bolong Beach. The self-serve menu is aimed at surfers and surfer-wannabes: burgers, pizza, fish and chips, salads. Wednesday nights are an institution, while Fridays (live rock and roll) and Sundays (DJs) are also big. (☑0361-846 9158; www.old-mans.net; Jl Pantai Batu Bolong; mains from 50,000Rp; ⏰7am-midnight)

Drinking

Potato Head
CLUB

12 MAP P64, D4

Bali's highest-profile beach club is also one of the best. Wander up off the sand or follow a long drive off Jl Petitenget and you'll find much to amuse, from an enticing pool to restaurants like the swanky Kaum and zero-waste Ijen, along with a pizza garden, lots of lounges and patches of lawn for chillin' the night away under the stars. (☑0361-473 7979; www.ptthead.com; Jl Petitenget 51; ⏰10am-2am; 🛜)

Mirror
CLUB

13 MAP P64, E4

This club is big with south Bali expats, who may own those designer shops you were in a few hours before. The interior is sort of like a cathedral out of Harry Potter, albeit with an unholy amount of lighting effects. Mainstream electronica blares forth. (☑0811 399 3010; www.mirror.id; Jl Petitenget 106; ⏰11pm-4am Wed-Sat)

La Brisa
INTERNATIONAL

14 MAP P64, A1

The newest member of Bali's trendy La family – which encompasses La Plancha, La Favela and

La Sicilia – La Brisa is nestled along the sands of Echo Beach in Canggu. Constructed using reclaimed wood from old fishing boats, this ocean-themed restaurant and bar is aptly decorated with fishing nets, fishing rods, seashells and antique buoys. (📞0811 394 6666; www.labrisabali.com; Jl Pantai Batu Mejan, Gang La Brisa; 🕐7am-11pm Mon-Sat, from 11am Sun; 📶)

Ji
BAR

15 🚍 MAP P64, B2

Easily Canggu's most alluring bar, Ji is a fantasy of historic Chinese and Balinese wood carving and rich decor. From the terrace on the 1st floor there are fine views you can enjoy with exotic cocktails,

sake and Japanese bites. (📞0361-473 1701; www.jiatbalesutra.com; Jl Pantai Batu Bolong, Hotel Tugu Bali; 🕐5-11pm)

40 Thieves
BAR

16 🚍 MAP P64, E3

A New York–style speakeasy, this hidden bar is perched above Mad Ronin, a Japanese ramen restaurant, in the trendy area of Seminyak. The atmospheric venue, which is peppered with memorabilia such as old maps and vintage bicycles, attracts a good mix of expats, tourists and locals. There is no signage, so enquire at Mad Ronin if you get lost. (📞0878 6226 7657; www.facebook.com/40thieves.bali; Jl Petitenget 7; 🕐8pm-2am Mon-Thu, to 4am Fri & Sat; 📶)

Potato Head

RADITYA / SHUTTERSTOCK ©

The Villa Life

Villas are scattered around south Bali and Ubud, and are now appearing in the east. They're often built in the middle of rice paddies, seemingly overnight. The villa boom has been quite controversial for environmental, aesthetic and economic reasons. Many skip collecting government taxes from guests, which has raised the ire of their luxury hotel competitors and brought threats of crackdowns.

Large villas, such as those in the Canggu area, can be bacchanalian retreats for groups of friends. Others are smaller, more intimate and part of larger developments – common in Seminyak and Kerobokan – or top-end hotels. Expect the following: a private garden and pool; a kitchen; air-con bedroom(s); and an open-air common space. Villas will also potentially include your own staff (cook, driver, cleaner), a private beachfront and isolation (which can be good or bad).

Rates range from around US$200 per night for a modest villa to US$2000 per week and beyond for your own tropical estate. There are often deals, especially in the low season, and several couples sharing can make something grand affordable.

You can sometimes save quite a bit by waiting until the last minute, but during the high season the best villas book up far in advance. Contact Bali Discovery (p146).

Shopping

Purpa Fine Art Gallery ART

17 🔒 MAP P64, F4

This long-time gallery has shown some of Bali's very best artists going back to the most notable names of the 1930s, such as Spies, Snell and Lempad. It has regular special exhibits. (📞0819 9940 8804; www.purpagallerybali.com; Jl Mertanadi 22; ⏰10am-6pm Mon-Sat)

Love Anchor MARKET

18 🔒 MAP P64, B1

Built in a traditional *joglo* style, this wood- and palm-tree-laden

Canggu village is the trifecta of hipster retail, food and shopping. You can kick back with a Bintang or fuel up on everything from pizzas and burgers to smoothies and vegan-friendly fare before browsing boutiques and surf shops. The open-air weekend bazaar (9am to 5pm Saturday and Sunday) is a one-stop shop for everything from Balinese souvenir essentials (circular rattan purse, anyone?) to chic custom leather goods and delicate jewellery hand-made by local artisans. (📞0822 3660 4648; www.loveanchorcanggu.com; Jl Pantai Batu Bolong 56; ⏰8am-midnight Mon-Fri, bazaar 9am-5pm Sat & Sun)

It Was All A Dream

FASHION & ACCESSORIES

19 🔒 MAP P64, D1

Great-quality leather bags, fun sunglasses, vintage jeans, jersey basics, embroidered kaftans and more. This hip boutique has original pieces at very reasonable prices. It's run by a French-American pair of expat designers. (📞0811 388 3322; Jl Pantai Berawa 14B; 🕙10am-7pm)

Dylan Board Store

SPORTS & OUTDOORS

20 🔒 MAP P64, B1

Famed big-wave rider Dylan Longbottom runs this custom surfboard shop. A talented shaper, he creates boards for novices and pros alike. He also stocks plenty of his own designs that are ready to go. (📞0819 9982 5654; www.dylan surfboards.com; Jl Pantai Batu Bolong; 🕙10am-8pm)

Explore

Jimbaran

Teluk Jimbaran (Jimbaran Bay) is an appealing crescent of white-sand beach and blue sea fronted by a long string of seafood warungs (food stalls) and ending at the southern end in a bushy headland, home to the Four Seasons Jimbaran Bay.

Despite increased popularity, Jimbaran remains a relaxed alternative to Kuta and Seminyak to the north (and just south of the airport, you can't beat the access!). Its markets offer a fascinating glimpse into local life.

The Short List

∘ **Jimbaran Beach (p75)** *Mellow surf and a vast selection of eateries make this beach one of Bali's best.*

∘ **Jimbaran Fish Market (p75)** *Bold and lively local market hawking every fresh catch imaginable.*

∘ **Seafood Restaurants (p77)** *Digging into fresh grilled seafood on the water's edge.*

Getting There & Around

🚗 Plenty of taxis wait around the beachfront warungs in the evening to take diners home (about 150,000Rp to Seminyak in no traffic). Some of the seafood warungs provide free transport if you call first. Ask for a flat fee on your transport if you travel during high traffic times, from 4pm to 8pm. Sundays are remarkably traffic-free.

🚌 The Kura-Kura tourist bus has a route linking Jimbaran with its Kuta hub. Buses run every two hours and cost 50,000Rp.

Jimbaran Map on p74

Tegalwangi Beach (p75) MICHELE FALZONE / GETTY IMAGES ©

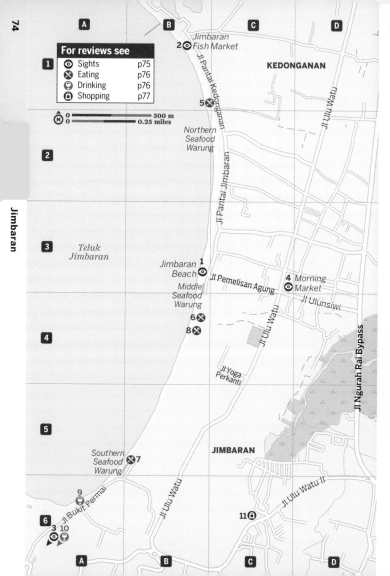

For reviews see

👁	Sights	p75
✗	Eating	p76
🍷	Drinking	p76
🛍	Shopping	p77

N
0 — 500 m
0 — 0.25 miles

KEDONGANAN

2 Jimbaran Fish Market

Jl Pantai Kedonganan

5

Northern Seafood Warung

Jl Pantai Jimbaran

Teluk Jimbaran

Jimbaran Beach 1

4 Morning Market

Jl Pemelisan Agung

Jl Ulunsiwi

Middle Seafood Warung

6

8

Jl Ulu Watu

Jl Yoga Perkanti

Jl Ngurah Rai Bypass

JIMBARAN

Southern Seafood Warung 7

9

Jl Bukit Permai

Jl Ulu Watu

Jl Ulu Watu II

11

6

3 10

A B C D

Sights

Jimbaran Beach
BEACH

1  MAP P74, B3

One of Bali's best beaches, Jimbaran's 4km-long arc of sand is mostly clean and there is no shortage of places to get a snack, drink or seafood dinner, or to rent a sunlounger. The bay is protected by an unbroken coral reef, which keeps the surf more mellow than at popular Kuta further north, although you can still get breaks that are fun for bodysurfing.

Jimbaran Fish Market
MARKET

2  MAP P74, B1

A popular morning stop on a Bukit peninsula amble, this fish market is smelly, lively and frenetic – watch where you step. Brightly painted boats bob along the shore while huge cases of everything from small sardines to fearsome langoustines are hawked. The action is fast and furious. Buy your seafood here and have one of the warungs cook it up or, for an even better price, buy direct from the boats between 6am and 7am. There's also a street vendor selling delicious sugar-cane juice for 10,000Rp. (Jimbaran Beach; ⏱6am-5pm)

Tegalwangi Beach
BEACH

3  MAP P74, A6

Folding around limestone bluffs some 4.5km southwest of Jimbaran, Tegalwangi is the first of cove after cove holding patches of beautiful sand all down the west coast of the peninsula. A

Jimbaran Beach

small parking area lies in front of Pura Segara Tegalwangi temple, a popular place for addressing the ocean gods. There's usually a lone drinks vendor offering refreshment before (or after) you make the short but challenging trip over the bad paths down to the beach. Immediately south, the vast Ayana Resort sprawls over the cliffs. From Jimbaran, take Jl Bukit Permai for 3km until the gates of the Ayana, where it veers west 1.5km to the temple.

Morning Market

MARKET

4 ◉ MAP P74, C3

This is one of the best markets in Bali for a visit because it's compact, so you can see a lot without wandering forever. Local chefs swear by the quality of the fruit and vegetables – ever seen a cabbage that big? (Jl Ulu Watu; ⏱6am-noon)

Eating

Jimbaran Bay Seafood

SEAFOOD $$

5 🍴 MAP P74, B1

The menu assures patrons that seeing the prices means 'Don't be worry!' Part of the rather staid northern group, JBS is especially welcoming with a huge variety of tables: inside under cover, on the concrete terrace or out where your toes can tickle the sand. (JBS; ☎0851-0172 5367; www.jimbaranbay seafoods.com; Jl Pantai Kedonganan; fresh seafood from 20,000Rp/100gr; ⏱11am-10pm)

Warung Ramayana

SEAFOOD $$

6 🍴 MAP P74, B4

Fishing boats dot the beach in front of this long-running favourite. The seafood marinates from the early morning and grills smoke all evening. The menu has useful fixed prices so you can avoid bargaining. (☎0361-702859; off Jl Pantai Jimbaran; mains from 80,000Rp; ⏱8am-11pm)

Made Bagus Cafe

SEAFOOD $$

7 🍴 MAP P74, B5

Tucked away at the north end of the southern group; the staff serving their narrow patch of tables on the beach here radiate charm. Go for one of the mixed platters and ask for extra sauce, it's that good. (☎0361-701858; off Jl Bukit Permai; meals 80,000-200,000Rp; ⏱8am-10.30pm)

Warung Bamboo

SEAFOOD $$

8 🍴 MAP P74, B4

Warung Bamboo is slightly more appealing than its neighbours, all of which have a certain raffish charm. The menu is dead simple: choose your seafood and the sides and sauces are included. (☎0361-702188; off Jl Pantai Jimbaran; meals 80,000-200,000Rp; ⏱10am-11pm)

Drinking

Jimbaran Beach Club

CAFE

9 🍺 MAP P74, A6

Just in case Jimbaran Bay wasn't inviting enough, this beach bar has

Jimbaran Seafood Restaurants

🍴

Jimbaran's three groups of seafood restaurants cook fresh, barbecued seafood every evening (most serve lunch as well), drawing tourists from across the south. Tables and chairs are set up on the sand almost to the water's edge. Arrive before sunset so you can get a good table and enjoy the show over a couple of beers before you dine.

Fixed prices for seafood platters in a plethora of varieties have become common and allow you to avoid the sport of choosing your fish and then paying for it by weight on scales that cause locals to break out in laughter. However, should you go this route, be sure to agree on costs first. Generally, you can enjoy a seafood feast, sides and a couple of beers for less than US$20 per person. Lobster (from US$30) will bump that figure up considerably, but you can keep the price low by purchasing your own lobster beforehand at the seafood market.

a long pool bordering the sand. It's rather upmarket: you can rent a comfy lounger and umbrella and enjoy ordering from a long drinks and food menu. (📞0361-709959; www.jimbaranbeachclub.com; Jl Bukit Permai Muaya; minimum spend 200,000Rp; ⏰8am-11pm; 📶)

Rock Bar
BAR

10 🚌 MAP P74, A6

Star of a thousand glossy articles written about Bali, this bar perched 14m above the crashing Indian Ocean is very popular. In fact, at sunset the wait to ride the lift down to the bar can top one hour. There's a no-backpacks, no-singlets dress code. The food is Med-flavoured bar snacks. (📞0361-702222; www.ayanaresort. com/rockbarbali; Jl Karang Mas Sejahtera, Ayana Resort; ⏰4pm-midnight, to 1am Fri & Sat; 📶)

Shopping

Jenggala Keramik Bali Ceramics
CERAMICS

11 🔒 MAP P74, C6

This modern warehouse showcases beautiful ceramic homewares that are a popular Balinese purchase. There's a viewing area where you can watch production, as well as a cafe. Ceramic courses are available for adults and children; a paint-a-pot scheme lets you create your own work of art (ready five days later after a trip through the kiln). (📞0361-703311; www.jenggala.com; Jl Ulu Watu II; ⏰8am-8pm)

Explore ⊚

Ulu Watu

Ulu Watu has become the generic name for the southwestern tip of the Bukit peninsula. It includes the much-revered temple and the fabled namesake surf breaks.

About 2km north of the temple there is a dramatic cliff with steps leading to the water and Suluban Beach. All manner of cafes and surf shops spill down the nearly sheer face to the water below. Views are stellar and it's quite the scene.

The Short List

○ **Pura Luhur Ulu Watu (p80)** *Appreciating intricate mythological carvings and taking in stunning views from this important seaside temple.*

○ **Ulu Watu (p83)** *Making a surfing sojourn to Bali's most legendary, powerful wave.*

○ **Single Fin (p87)** *Gazing over endless, hypnotic swells with a sunset cocktail.*

○ **Omnia (p86)** *Dancing the day away by the infinity pool at this clifftop day club overlooking the Indian Ocean.*

Getting There & Around

🚗 **Car & Motorcycle** The best way to see the Ulu Watu region is with your own wheels. Note that the cops often set up checkpoints near Pecatu Indah for checks on motorcycle-riding Westerners. Be aware you may pay a fine for offences such as a 'loose' chin strap.

🚕 A taxi ride out here will cost at least 200,000Rp from Kuta and takes more than an hour in traffic.

Ulu Watu Map on p82

Bar overlooking Suluban Beach (p83) AARON LIM / SHUTTERSTOCK ©

Top Experience 📷

Get Spiritual at Pura Luhur Ulu Watu

*This important temple is perched precipitously
on the southwestern tip of the peninsula, atop
sheer cliffs that drop straight into the cease-
less surf. You enter through an unusual arched
gateway flanked by statues of Ganesha. Inside,
the walls of coral bricks are covered with intricate
carvings of Bali's mythological menagerie.*

◉ MAP P82, B4

off Jl Ulu Watu

adult/child
30,000/20,000Rp,
parking 2000Rp

🕖 7am-7pm

Only Hindu worshippers can enter the small inner temple that is built onto the jutting tip of land. However, the views of the endless swells of the Indian Ocean from the cliffs are almost spiritual. At sunset, walk around the clifftop to the left (south) of the temple to lose some of the crowd.

Ulu Watu is one of several important temples to the spirits of the sea along the south coast of Bali. In the 11th century the Javanese priest Empu Kuturan first established a temple here. The complex was added to by Nirartha, another Javanese priest who is known for the seafront temples at Tanah Lot, Rambut Siwi and Pura Sakenan. Nirartha retreated to Ulu Watu for his final days when he attained *moksa* (freedom from earthly desires).

Kecak Dance

Pura Luhur Ulu Watu's daily sunset *kecak* and fire dance performances (p87), though geared towards tourists, are a beautiful and fascinating highlight. Kecak developed from an ancient Balinese ritual known as *sanghyang*, a trance-like dance fuelled by repetitive chanting, which in its ancient form channelled the wishes of gods and ancestors. Performed in the temple's ampitheatre, the trance-inducing show features a circle of bare-chested men chanting in rhythmic unison as the sun sets. It culminates in a dramatic fire show that is integral to the Ramayana narrative – a synopsis of the story is handed out to audience members so you won't miss a detail.

★ Top Tips

o The temple's monkeys have notoriously kleptomaniac tendencies – hats, jewellery and glasses are all too easy for them to snatch. If one absconds with your belongings, they can usually be persuaded to trade it back for a piece of fruit (locals are willing to take care of it for you in exchange for a small tip).

✕ Take a Break

Head to Single Fin (p87) for a bite with amazing views of Bali's most famous surf break.

Omnia (p86) day club offers a stark contrast of blissful sin to Pura Luhur Ulu Watu's serenity.

Ulu Watu

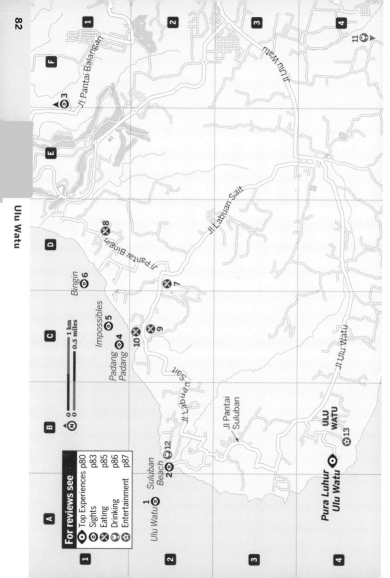

For reviews see
- ◉ Top Experiences p80
- ◎ Sights p83
- ✕ Eating p85
- ◉ Drinking p86
- ✿ Entertainment p87

Jl Pantai Balangan

◉3

Jl Ulu Watu

⦿11

Jl Labuan Sait

Bingin ◎6

✕◉8

Jl Pantai Bingin

✕7

Impossibles ◎5

Padang Padang ◎4

✕10

✕9

Jl Labuan Sait

Jl Labuan Sait

Jl Ulu Watu

Suluban Beach

Ulu Watu ◉1

◎⦿12

2◎

Jl Pantai Suluban

ULU WATU
✿13

Pura Luhur Ulu Watu ◉

0   1 km
0   0.5 miles

Sights

Ulu Watu
SURFING

1 MAP P82, A2

On its day Ulu Watu is Bali's biggest and most powerful wave. It's the stuff of dreams and nightmares, and definitely not one for beginners! Since the early 1970s when it featured in the legendary surf flick *Morning of the Earth*, Ulu Watu has drawn surfers from around the world for left breaks that seem to go on forever.

Suluban Beach
BEACH

2 MAP P82, B2

While others paddle out to the Ulu Watu surf breaks, you can linger on this strip of sand in an uberdramatic setting: limestone cliffs and caves surround the beach. Check the tides before making the steep climb down.

Balangan
SURFING

3 MAP P82, F1

Off the long strip of sand that is Balangan Beach, the namesake surf break is a fast left over a shallow reef, unsurfable at low tide and good at midtide with anything over a 4ft swell; with an 8ft swell, this is one of the classic waves.

Padang Padang
SURFING

4 MAP P82, C1

Padang for short, this super-shallow, left-hand reef break is off a very popular beach and just below some rickety accommodation joints where you can crash and

Surfing at Balangan

MARIUS DOBILAS / SHUTTERSTOCK ©

Responsible Travel

To visit Bali responsibly, tread lightly as you go, with respect for both the land and the culture of its people.

Watch your use of water Water demand outstrips supply, even at seemingly green places like Bali. Take your hotel up on its offer to save water by not washing your sheets and towels every day. At the high end you can also forgo your own private plunge pool, or a pool altogether.

Don't hit the bottle Those bottles of water are convenient but they add up. The zillions tossed away each year are a serious blight. Since tap water is unsafe, ask your hotel if you can refill from their huge containers of drinking water. Some enlightened businesses already offer this service.

Support environmentally aware businesses The number of businesses committed to good environmental practices is growing fast.

Conserve power Turn off lights and air-con when not using them.

Bag the bags Refuse plastic bags and plastic straws, too.

Leave animals be Reconsider swimming with captive dolphins, riding elephants and patronising attractions where wild animals are made to perform for crowds – such interactions have been identified by animal welfare experts as harmful to the animals. Don't try to pet, feed or otherwise interact with animals in the wild as it disrupts their natural behaviour and can make them sick.

watch the breaks. Check carefully before venturing out. It's a demanding break that only works if it's over about 6ft from mid- to high tide.

Impossibles
SURFING

5 ◉ MAP P82, C1

Just north of Padang Padang, this challenging outside reef break has three shifting peaks with fast left-hand tube sections that can join up if the conditions are perfect.

Bingin
SURFING

6 ◉ MAP P82, D1

Given the walk down to Bingin Beach from the isolated parking area, you could be forgiven if you decide to leave your board up top, but don't. Waves here are best at midtide with a 6ft swell when short but perfect left-hand barrels form, and you'll do well to have somebody onshore recording your action.

Eating

Bukit Cafe
AUSTRALIAN $

7 🍽 MAP P82, D2

For heaping plates of Australian-style brunch composed of fresh, local ingredients, Bukit Cafe is unbeatable. Standout dishes include vegan pancakes, smoothie bowls and smashed avocado, and the open-air, convivial setting has loads of appeal. (📞0822 3620 8392; www.bukitcafe.com; Jl Labuan Sait; mains 40,000-75,000Rp; ⏰7am-10pm; 🍴)

Cashew Tree
CAFE $

8 🍽 MAP P82, D1

The place to hang out in Bingin. Surfers and beachgoers gather in this large garden for tasty vegetarian meals. Expect the likes of burritos, salads, sandwiches and smoothies – it's also a good spot for a drink. Thursday nights especially go off, with live bands attracting folk from up and down the coast. (📞0813 5321 8157; www.facebook.com/thecashewtreebingin; Jl Pantai Bingin; meals from 55,000Rp; ⏰8am-10pm; 📶🍴)

Mango Tree Cafe
CAFE $$

9 🍽 MAP P82, C2

This two-level cafe has a long menu of healthy options. Sandwiches and the tasty burgers have amazing buns. The salads, soups, breakfast burritos and more are fresh and interesting. There are good juices and a decent drinks

Kecak performance, Pura Luhur Ulu Watu (p80)

Bali's Landscape

Bali sits midway along the Indonesian archipelago, adjacent to the island of Java and immediately west of the chain of smaller islands comprising Nusa Tenggara, which includes Lombok. It's visually dramatic and mountainous, with a string of active volcanoes and peaks around 2000m. Agricultural lands are south and north of the central mountains; the southern region is a wide, gently sloping area, where most of Indonesia's rice crop is grown. The northern coastal strip is narrower, rising into the foothills of the central range. It receives less rain, but coffee, copra, rice and cattle are farmed there. Arid, less-populated regions include the western mountain region, and the eastern and northeastern slopes of Gunung Agung. The Nusa Penida islands are dry and cannot support intensive agriculture. The Bukit peninsula is similarly dry, but with the growth of tourism, it's become very populous. From pearly hidden coves to sparkling black sweeps, and lonely strands to party scenes, Bali has beaches in all shapes, characters and colours.

list. Try for a table under the namesake tree. The owner, Maria, is a generous delight. (☎0878-6246-6763; Jl Labuan Sait 17; mains 60,000-120,000Rp; ☻7am-11pm)

Om Burger
BURGERS $$

10 🍽 MAP P82, C2

'Superfood burgers' – that's the come-on at this joint with nice 2nd-floor views. The burgers are indeed super and supersized. The shaka burger (with Wagyu beef) is the speciality, but the nasi goreng veggie burger is unique. There are intimations of health across the menu: baked sweet-potato fries, vitamin-filled juices and more. (☎0819 9905 5232; Jl Labuan Sait; mains from 55,000Rp, burgers from 75,000Rp; ☻7am-10pm; 🛜))

Drinking

Omnia
CLUB

11 🕒 MAP P82, F4

Perched at the base of the Bukit peninsula, Bali's hottest new day club is home to seekers of sunshine-fuelled revelry and house and hip-hop beats. The imposing architecture of the modern Cube bar is a stunning focal point, but a peek over its patio's glass barriers yields an eyeful of jagged cliffs, lush oceanside canopy and hypnotic azure waves.

There's an impressive infinity pool that blends into a seamless panorama of the Indian Ocean, fringed with plush sun loungers. Cocktails are inventive and the food spans a broad range of cuisines and preparations. This playground is for adults only (21+). Reservations recommended. (📞0361-848 2150; https://omnia clubs.com/bali; Jl Belimbing Sari; cover charge varies by day & event, check website for details; 🕐11am-10.30pm)

Single Fin

BAR

12 🚇 MAP P82, B2

From this triple-level cafe, you can watch never-ending swells march across the Indian Ocean from this cliff-side perch, and the surfers carve it up when the waves are big. Drinks here aren't cheap (or very good), but the food (mains 65,000Rp to 165,000Rp) is tasty, the sunsets are killer and the Sunday night party is the best on the peninsula. An attached poke-bowl joint, Coco & Poke, is under the same ownership. The bowls start at 75,000Rp and are available from 11am to 7pm Monday through Saturday, and to 9pm Sunday. There's a tofu bowl for vegetarians. (📞0361-769941; www. singlefinbali.com; Jl Mamo; 🕐8am-9pm Mon-Sat, to 1am Sun; 🛜)

Entertainment

Kecak Dance

DANCE

13 ⭐ MAP P82, B4

Although the performance obviously caters for tourists, the gorgeous setting at Pura Luhur Ulu Watu (p80) in a small amphitheatre in a leafy part of the grounds makes it one of the more evocative on the island.

The views out to sea are as inspiring as the dance. It's very popular during high season; expect crowds and book ahead. (Pura Luhur Ulu Watu, off Jl Ulu Watu; 100,000Rp; 🕐sunset)

Explore ◈

Nusa Dua
& Tanjung Benoa

Built in the 1970s to compete with international beach resorts, Bali's gated compound of Nusa Dua is a vast and manicured place where you leave the chaos of the rest of the island behind as you pass the guards. The adjacent peninsula of Tanjung Benoa is lined with midrange family-friendly resort hotels, where waters buzz with the roar of dozens of motorised water-sports craft.

The Short List

○ **Pasifika Museum (p91)** *Exploring the artistic works of Pacific Ocean cultures from centuries over.*

○ **Beach Promenade (p91)** *Ambling past crystalline waters that stretch the length of Nusa Dua up through Tanjung Benoa.*

○ **Bumbu Bali Cooking School (p92)** *Rising early to source ingredients from morning markets before trying your hand at Balinese culinary traditions.*

Getting There & Around

🚌 A free shuttle bus connects Nusa Dua and Tanjung Benoa resort hotels with the Bali Collection shopping centre about every hour. The Kura-Kura tourist bus has two routes linking Nusa Dua with its Kuta hub.

🚕 A taxi from the airport cartel is 150,000Rp to Nusa Dua and 200,000Rp to Tanjung Benoa; a metered taxi to the airport will be much less. Taxis to/from Seminyak average 150,000Rp for the 45-minute trip, although traffic can double this time.

Nusa Dua & Tanjung Benoa Map on p90

Sunrise from Tanjung Benoa RANDI_LANG / SHUTTERSTOCK ©

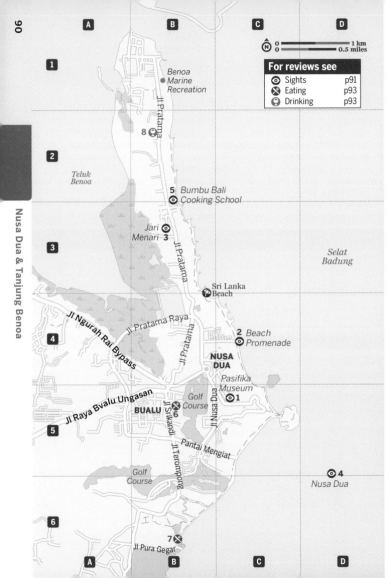

For reviews see

◉ Sights p91
✖ Eating p93
🍷 Drinking p93

0 — 1 km
0 — 0.5 miles

Benoa Marine Recreation

Jl Pratama

8 ◉

Teluk Benoa

5 ◉ Bumbu Bali Cooking School

Jl Pratama

Jari Menari 3 ◉

Selat Badung

◉ Sri Lanka Beach

Jl Pratama Raya

2 ◉ Beach Promenade

Jl Ngurah Rai Bypass

Jl Pratama

NUSA DUA

Pasifika Museum
◉ 1

Jl Raya Bvalu Ungasan

BUALU

Golf Course

✖ 6
Jl Srikandi

Jl Nusa Dua

Pantai Mengiat

Jl Terompong

Golf Course

◉ 4
Nusa Dua

6

7 ✖

Jl Pura Gegar

Sights

Pasifika Museum

MUSEUM

1 ◎ MAP P90, C5

When groups from nearby resorts aren't around, you'll probably have this large museum to yourself. A collection of art from Pacific Ocean cultures spans several centuries and includes more than 600 paintings (don't miss the tikis). The influential wave of European artists who thrived in Bali in the early 20th century is well represented. Look for works by Arie Smit, Adrien-Jean Le Mayeur de Merpres and Theo Meier. There are also works by Matisse and Gauguin. (📞0361-774935; www.museum-pasifika.com; Bali Collection shopping centre, block P; 100,000Rp; ⏱10am-6pm)

Beach Promenade

WALKING

2 ◎ MAP P90, C4

One of the nicest features of Nusa Dua is the 5km-long beach promenade that stretches the length of the resort from Pura Gegar in the south and north along much of the beach through Tanjung Benoa.

Jari Menari

SPA

3 ◎ MAP P90, B3

This branch of the famed Seminyak original offers all the same exquisite massages by the expert all-male staff. Call for transport. (📞0361-778084; www.jarimenari nusadua.com; Jl Pratama; massage from 435,000Rp; ⏱9am-10pm)

Dishes from Bumbu Bali 1 (p93)

Water Sports

Water-sports centres along Jl Pratama offer daytime diving, cruises, windsurfing and waterskiing. Each morning convoys of buses arrive with day trippers from all over south Bali, and by 10am parasailers float over the water. All the centres feature unctuous salespeople whose job it is to sell you the banana-boat ride of your dreams while you sit in a thatched-roof sales centre and cafe. Check equipment and credentials, as a few tourists have died in accidents.

Among the established water-sports operators is **Benoa Marine Recreation** (BMR; Map p90, B1; ☎0361-772438; www.bmrbali.com; Jl Pratama; ☉8am-4pm). All operators have similar prices. Note that 'official' price lists are just the starting point for bargaining.

Activities here include the following (with average prices).

Banana-boat rides Wild rides for two as you try to maintain your grasp on the inflatable fruit moving over the waves (US$25 per 15 minutes).

Glass-bottomed boat trips The non-wet way to see the denizens of the shallows (US$50 per hour).

Jet-skiing Go fast and belch smoke (US$30 per 15 minutes).

Parasailing Iconic; you float above the water while being towed by a speedboat (US$25 per 15-minute trip).

Snorkelling Trips include equipment and a boat ride to a reef (US$40 per hour).

Nusa Dua
SURFING

4 ◉ MAP P90, D5

During wet season, the reef off Nusa Dua has very consistent swells. The main break is 1km off the beach to the south of Nusa Dua – off Gegar Beach (where you can get a boat out to the break for 200,000Rp).

There are lefts and rights that work well on a small swell at low to midtide.

Bumbu Bali Cooking School
COOKING

5 ◉ MAP P90, B2

This much-lauded cooking school at the restaurant of the same name strives to get to the roots of Balinese cooking. Courses start with a 6am visit to Jimbaran's fish market and morning market, continue in the large kitchen and then finish with lunch. (☎0361-774502; www.balifoods.com; Jl

Pratama; course with/without market visit US$95/85; ⏰6am-3pm Mon, Wed & Fri)

Eating

Bumbu Bali 1 BALINESE $$

Long-time resident and cookbook author Heinz von Holzen, his wife Puji, and their well-trained and enthusiastic staff serve exquisitely flavoured dishes at this superb restaurant (see 5 ◎ Map p90). Many diners opt for one of several lavish set menus. Cooking classes on Monday, Wednesday and Friday (from US$85) are highly recommended. (📞0361-774502; www.balifoods.com; Jl Pratama; mains from 100,000Rp, set menus from 325,000Rp; ⏰noon-9pm)

Warung Dobiel BALINESE $

6 ✖ MAP P90, B5

A bit of authentic food action amid the bland streets of Nusa, this is a good stop for *babi guling* (spit-roast pig). Pork soup is the perfect taste bud awakener, while the jack-fruit is redolent with spices. Diners perch on stools and share tables; service can be slow and tours

may mob the place. Watch out for 'foreigner' pricing. (📞0361-771633; Jl Srikandi 9; meals from 40,000Rp; ⏰9am-4pm)

Nusa Dua Beach Grill INTERNATIONAL $$

7 ✖ MAP P90, B6

A good spot for day trippers, this warm-hued cafe (hidden by the Mulia resort) is just south of Gegar Beach. The drinks menu is long, the seafood fresh and the relaxed beachy vibe intoxicating. (📞0851 0043 4779; www.nusaduabeachgrill.com; Jl Pura Gegar; mains from 85,000Rp; ⏰8am-10.30pm)

Drinking

Atlichnaya Bar BAR

8 🍺 MAP P90, B2

A lively and convivial alternative to the stiff hotel bars, this rollicking place serves a long list of cheap mixed drinks and even offers massages (from 50,000Rp). There are cheap and cheery Indo and Western menu items as well. (📞0813 3818 9675; www.atlichnaya.com; Jl Pratama 88; ⏰8am-late; 🛜)

Explore

Sanur

Many consider Sanur 'just right', as it lacks most of the hassles found to the west while maintaining a good mix of restaurants and bars that aren't all owned by resorts. The beach, while thin, is protected by a reef and breakwaters, so families appreciate the limpid waves. Sanur has a good range of places to stay and it's well placed for day trips.

The Short List

○ **Sanur Beachfront (p96)** *Ambling past beachfront cafes, wooden fishing boats and elegant villas along Bali's original beach promenade.*

○ **Museum Le Mayeur (p99)** *Admiring Balinese-style architecture housing vibrant works by artist Adrien-Jean Le Mayeur de Merpres.*

○ **Taman Festival Bali (p99)** *Taking in the ghost-town-like atmosphere at this abandoned amusement park.*

Getting There & Around

🚕 A cartel of taxis at the airport has a set price of 250,000Rp to Sanur.

🚌 The Kura-Kura tourist bus has a route linking Sanur with Kuta and Ubud. Buses run every hour and cost 80,000Rp.

Sanur Map on p98

Bali Kite Festival (p101), Pantai Padang Galak

Walking Tour 🥾

Sanur's Beachfront Walk

Sanur's beachfront walk has been delighting locals and visitors alike from day one. More than 4km long, it curves past resorts, cafes, fishing boats and elegant villas built decades ago by wealthy expats who fell under Bali's spell. While you stroll, look out across the water to Nusa Penida. Even if you're not staying in Sanur, the beach walk makes a good day trip or stop on the way to someplace else.

Start Museum Le Mayeur

End Fairmont Sanur Beach Resort

Length 4km; 1 to 1½ hours

Follow this Beachfront Walk for a wide choice of places to sit down with a drink and beach view. Although sunset drink specials are common, the beach faces east. (You can still enjoy the reflected glow off Nusa Penida.)

❶ Grand Bali Beach Hotel

Built in the Sukarno era, this vast **hotel** (Jl Hang Tuah) is now slowly fading away. Local leaders, properly horrified at its outsized bulk, imposed the famous rule that no building could be higher than a coconut palm.

❷ Turtle Tanks

An engaging **display** about Bali's endangered sea turtles that usually includes some young hatchlings.

❸ Pura Patal Temple

Amid the tourist bustle, this little **shrine** is shaded by huge trees.

❹ Batu Jimbar

Just north of the old Hyatt (awaiting a grand makeover at the time of writing), this **villa compound** (📞0361 737498; www.villabatujimbar.

Worth a Detour

Down a narrow lane off Jl Danau Poso and to the left as you face Pura Belangjong, is Bali's oldest dated artefact – a stone pillar – with ancient inscriptions recounting military victories from more than a thousand years ago. These inscriptions are in Sanskrit and are evidence of Hindu influence 300 years before the arrival of the Majapahit court.

com; Beachfront Walk; villas from US$1400) has a colourful history. It was redesigned by the famous Sri Lankan architect Geoffrey Bawa in 1975, Mick Jagger and Jerry Hall were unofficially married here in 1990, and it has accommodated celebrities from Yoko Ono to Sting to Fergie. If your income approaches theirs, you too can stay here.

❺ Wooden Fishing Boats

Just south of the old Hyatt is a long area where multihued **fishing boats** are pulled ashore and repaired under the trees.

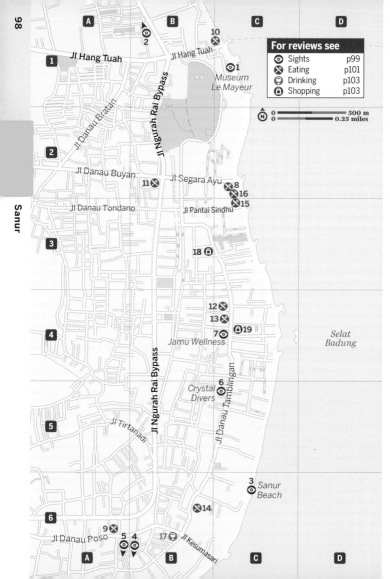

For reviews see
- ⊙ Sights — p99
- ✗ Eating — p101
- 🍷 Drinking — p103
- 🛍 Shopping — p103

0 — 500 m
0 — 0.25 miles

Jl Hang Tuah

Jl Hang Tuah

10 ✗

1 ⊙
Museum
Le Mayeur

Jl Ngurah Rai Bypass

Jl Danau Bratan

Jl Danau Buyan

11 ✗   Jl Segara Ayu

8 ✗
16 ✗
15 ✗

Jl Danau Tondano   Jl Pantai Sindhu

18 🛍

12 ✗
13 ✗
7 ⊙   🛍 19
Jamu Wellness

Selat
Badung

Jl Ngurah Rai Bypass

6 ⊙
Crystal
Divers

Jl Danau Tamblingan

Jl Tirtanadi

3 ⊙ Sanur
Beach

✗ 14

9 ✗
Jl Danau Poso   5   4
17 🍷   Jl Kesumasari

Sights

Museum Le Mayeur

MUSEUM

1 🔘 MAP P98, C1

Artist Adrien-Jean Le Mayeur de Merpres (1880–1958) arrived in Bali in 1932, and married the beautiful Legong dancer Ni Polok three years later, when she was just 15. They lived in this compound back when Sanur was still a quiet fishing village. After the artist's death, Ni Polok lived in the house until she died in 1985. Despite security (some of Le Mayeur's paintings have sold for US$150,000) and conservation problems, almost 90 of Le Mayeur's paintings are displayed. (☎0361-286201; Jl Hang Tuah; adult/child 50,000/25,000Rp; ⏱8am-3.30pm Sat-Thu, 8.30am-12.30pm Fri)

Taman Festival Bali

AMUSEMENT PARK

2 🔘 MAP P98, B1

One of the more unusual Bali attractions, Taman Festival Bali is an abandoned theme park about a 20-minute drive north of Sanur. Some say that the 8-hectare park closed its doors in 2000 after its $5 million laser equipment was struck by lightning, but it is more likely that the park closed due to the Asian economic crisis. (Jalan Padang Galak 3)

Abandoned theme park Taman Festival Bali

Sanur Beach
BEACH

3 ⊙ MAP P98, C6

Sanur Beach curves in a south-westerly direction and stretches for more than 5km. It is mostly clean and overall quite serene – much like the town itself. Offshore reefs mean that the surf is reduced to tiny waves lapping the shore. With a couple of unfortunate exceptions, the resorts along the sand are low-key, leaving the beach uncrowded.

Rip Curl School of Surf
KITESURFING

4 ⊙ MAP P98, B6

Sanur's reef-protected waters and regular offshore breezes make for good kitesurfing. The season runs from June to October. Rip Curl also rents boards for windsurfing and stand-up paddle boarding (including SUP yoga for 450,000Rp per hour) as well as kayaks. (☎0361-287749; www.ripcurlschoolofsurf.com; Beachfront Walk, Sanur Beach Hotel; kitesurfing lessons from 1,100,000Rp, rental per hour from 550,000Rp; ⏰8am-5pm)

Power of Now Oasis
YOGA

5 ⊙ MAP P98, A6

Enjoy a yoga class in this atmospheric bamboo pavilion looking out to Sanur Beach. Several levels are offered. Sunrise yoga is a popular choice. (☎0878 6153 4535; www.powerofnowoasis.com; Beachfront Walk, Hotel Mercure; classes from 120,000Rp)

Sanur Beach

Crystal Divers

DIVING

6 ⊚ MAP P98, C5

This slick diving operation has its own hotel (the Santai) and a large diving pool. The shop offers a long list of courses, including PADI open-water (7,450,000Rp) and options for beginners. (☏0361-286737; www.crystal-divers.com; Jl Danau Tamblingan 168; dives from 890,000Rp)

Jamu Wellness

SPA

7 ⊚ MAP P98, C4

This gracious spa has classy digs and offers a range of treatments including a popular Earth and Flower Body Mask and a Kemiri Nut Scrub. (☏0811 389 9930; www. jamuwellnessbali.com; Jl Danau Tamblingan 140; 1hr massage 195,000Rp; ⊙9am-9pm)

Eating

Nasi Bali Men Weti

BALINESE $

8 ✖ MAP P98, C2

This simple stall prepares excellent *nasi campur,* the classic Balinese lunch plate of mixed dishes. Everything is very fresh and prepared while you wait in the inevitable queue. Enjoy your meal perched on a small plastic stool. (Jl Segara Ayu; meals from 25,000Rp; ⊙7am-1pm)

Sari Bundo

INDONESIAN $

9 ✖ MAP P98, A6

This spotless Padang-style shopfront is one of several at the south end of Sanur. Choose from

Kite-flying Over Sanur

Travelling through south Bali you can't help but notice scores of huge, high-flying kites overhead much of the year. Many have noisemakers producing eerie buzzing noises unique to each kite. Like many things in Bali, there are spiritual roots: the kites are meant to whisper figuratively into the ears of the gods suggestions that abundant harvests might be nice. Each July, hundreds of Balinese and international teams descend on open spaces north of Sanur for the Bali Kite Festival. The action is centred around flat land behind the sand at Pantai Padang Galak, about 1km up the coast from Sanur. You can catch kite-flying Balinese-style here from May to September.

an array of fresh and very spicy food. The curry chicken is a fiery treat that will have your tongue alternatively loving and hating you. (☏0361-281389; Jl Danau Poso; mains from 20,000Rp; ⊙24hr)

Warung Mak Beng

BALINESE $

10 ✖ MAP P98, C1

You don't need a menu at this local favourite: all you can order is its legendary barbecued fish (*ikan laut goreng*), which comes with various sides and some tasty soup. Service is quick, the air fragrant and diners of all stripes are very happy. (📞0361-282633; Jl Hang Tuah 45; meals 35,000Rp; 🕐8am-9pm)

Warung Babi Guling Sanur

BALINESE $

11 ❌ MAP P98, B2

Unlike many of Bali's *babi guling* (spit-roast pig) places that buy their suckling pigs precooked from large suppliers, this small outlet does all its cooking right out back. The meat is succulent and shows the benefits of personal attention. (📞0361-287308; Jl Ngurah Rai Bypass; mains from 25,000Rp; 🕐10am-10pm)

Porch

CAFE $

12 ❌ MAP P98, C4

Housed in a traditional wooden building, this cafe offers a tasty mix of comfort food like burgers and freshly baked goods such as ciabatta. Snuggle up to a table on the porch or shut it all out in the air-con inside. Popular for breakfast; there's a long list of fresh juices. High tea is popular too (150,000Rp for two). (📞0361-281682; www. flashbacks-chb.com; Jl Danau Tamblingan 111, Flashbacks; mains from 50,000Rp; 🕐7am-10pm; ❄🛜)

Three Monkeys Cafe

ASIAN $$

13 ❌ MAP P98, C4

This branch of the Ubud original is no mere knock-off. It's spread over two floors, there's cool jazz playing in the background and live performances some nights. Set well back from the road, you can enjoy excel-

lent coffee on sofas or chairs. The menu mixes Western fare with pan-Asian creations. (📞0361-286002; www.threemonkeyscafebali.com; Jl Danau Tamblingan; mains 62,000-199,000Rp; 🕐11am-11pm; 🛜)

Char Ming

ASIAN $$

14 ❌ MAP P98, B6

Asian fusion with a French accent. A daily menu board lists the fresh seafood available for grilling. Look for regional dishes, many with modern flair. The highly stylised location features lush plantings and carved-wood details from vintage Javanese and Balinese structures. (📞0361-288029; www.charming-bali. com; Jl Danau Tamblingan N97; mains from 95,000Rp; 🕐5-11pm)

Byrdhouse Beach Club

INTERNATIONAL $$

15 ❌ MAP P98, C3

With loungers, a swimming pool, a restaurant, bar and table tennis on-site, you could happily spend an entire day here by the beach. Check the club's Facebook page for upcoming events, including outdoor-cinema screenings and street-food stalls. (📞0361-288407; www. facebook.com/byrdhousebeachclubbali; Segara Village, Sanur Beach; mains from 60,000Rp; 🕐6am-midnight; 🛜)

Minami

JAPANESE $$

16 ❌ MAP P98, C2

With its minimalist white decor, bright open-air atmosphere and a vast range of uberfresh fish,

Weaving ikat

this authentic Japanese place is a great find on Sanur Beach. (☏0812 8613 4471; Beachfront Walk; mains from 60,000Rp; ◷10am-11pm)

Drinking

Fire Station   PUB

17 🚇 MAP P98, B6

There's some old Hollywood style here at this open-fronted pub. Hollywood-esque portraits line walls; you expect to see a young Dennis Hopper lurking in the rear. Enjoy pitchers of sangria and other interesting drinks along with a varied menu of good pub food (mains from 99,000Rp) that features many specials. Order the fine Belgian beer, Duvel. (☏0361-285675; Jl Danau Poso 108; ◷4pm-late)

Shopping

Ganesha Bookshop   BOOKS

18 🔒 MAP P98, B3

A branch of Bali's best bookshop for serious readers. (☏0361-970320; www.ganeshabooksbali.com; Jl Danau Tamblingan 42; ◷10am-6pm)

A-Krea   CLOTHING

19 🔒 MAP P98, C4

An excellent spot for souvenirs, A-Krea has a range of items designed and made in Bali in its attractive store. Clothes, accessories, homewares,woven items and more are all handmade. (☏0361-286101; Jl Danau Tamblingan 51; ◷9am-9pm)

Worth a Trip 👓
Relax on Laid-Back Nusa Lembongan

Once the domain of shack-staying surfers, Nusa Lembongan has hit the big time. Yes, you can still get a simple room with a view of the surf breaks and the gorgeous sunsets, but now you can also stay in a boutique hotel and have a fabulous meal. But even as Nusa Lembongan's popularity grows, it maintains a mellow vibe.

Getting There

🚢 Sanur to Jungutbatu Beach (10 daily; 30 mins) including **Rocky Fast Cruises** (www.rockyfast cruise.com; one way/return 300,000/500,000Rp) and **Scoot** (www.scootcruise. com; adult/child one way 400,000/280,000Rp).

Jungutbatu Beach

A mostly lovely arc of white sand with clear blue water, this beach has views across to Gunung Agung in Bali. The pleasant seawall walkway is ideal for strolling, especially – as you'd guess – at sunset. Floating boats save the scene from being an idyllic cliché.

Mushroom Bay

Beautiful Tanjung Sanghyang, unofficially named Mushroom Bay after the mushroom corals offshore, has a crescent of bright white beach. The most interesting way to get here from Jungutbatu is to walk along the trail that starts from the southern end of the main beach and follows the coastline for a kilometre or so.

Surfing

Surfing here is best in dry season (April to September), when the winds come from the southeast. It's not for beginners and can be dangerous even for experts. There are three main breaks on the reef, all aptly named. From north to south are Shipwrecks, Lacerations and Playgrounds. A reputable local instruction outfit is **Thabu Surf Lessons** (☏ 0812 4620 2766; http://thabusurflessons.webs.com; adult/child based on skill level & group size from 450,000/400,000Rp).

Diving & Snorkelling

Nusa Lembongan is a good base for divers and the number of dive shops is proliferating. **World Diving** (☏ 0812 390 0686; www.world-diving.com; Jungutbatu Beach; introductory dive 940,000Rp, open-water course 5,500,000Rp) is very well regarded. Good snorkelling can be had just off Tanjung Sanghyang and the Bounty Pontoon, as well as in areas off the north coast of the island. You can charter a boat from about 200,000Rp per hour, depending on demand.

★ **Top Tips**

○ At the north end of town where the island's main road passes, you can ascend a long stone staircase to Pura Puseh, the village temple. It has great views from its hilltop location. Look for the enormous sacred tree.

○ Much of Nusa Lembongan faces Bali and enjoys spectacular sunsets; come 6pm, pick your favourite venue for a sundowner.

✕ **Take a Break**

There are numerous beach cafes with all the usual standards plus fabulous views. Tucked into a lovely garden on a side street off Jungutbatu Beach, **Green Garden Warung** (☏ 0813 374 1928; Jungutbatu; mains 20,000-50,000Rp; ⏰ 7am-10pm; ✏) serves up tasty smoothie bowls and creative Indonesian dishes, many of which are vegetarian friendly.

Explore ◈
Denpasar

Denpasar might not be a tropical paradise, but it's as much a part of 'the real Bali' as the rice paddies and clifftop temples. This is the hub of the island for nearly a million locals and here you will find their shopping malls and parks. Most enticing, however, are the authentic restaurants and cafes aimed at the burgeoning middle class.

The Short List

o *Bajra Sandhi Monument (p109)* Contemplating Hindu symbolism and the Balinese struggle for independence at this significant monument.

o *Museum Negeri Propinsi Bali (p109)* Taking in a wealth of cultural relics at Bali's oldest and largest museum.

o *Pura Jagatnatha (p110)* Appreciating the intricate carvings at the state temple dedicated to supreme Hindu god Sanghyang Widi.

Getting There & Around

🚌 Long-distance bus services use the Ubung Bus & Bemo Terminal, well north of town. Most long-distance services also stop at the Mengwi terminal.

🚗 The cabs of Blue Bird Taxi are the most reliable choice.

Denpasar Map on p108

Bajra Sandhi Monument (p109) RM NUNES / SHUTTERSTOCK ©

Denpasar

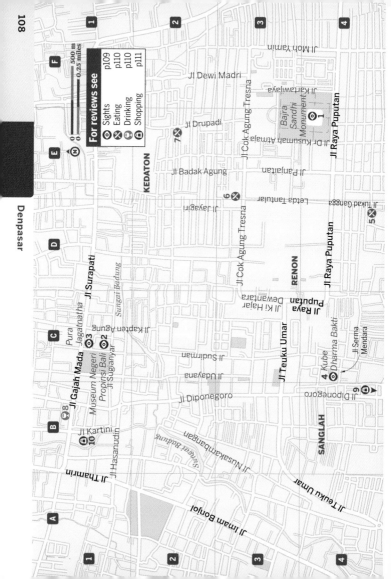

For reviews see

● Sights	p109
❸ Eating	p110
❶ Drinking	p110
❸ Shopping	p111

0 ————— 500 m
0 ————— 0.25 miles

KEDATON

RENON

SANGLAH

Jl Dewi Madri

Jl Drupadi

Jl Cok Agung Tresna

Jl Badak Agung

Jl Jayagiri

Jl Moh Yamin

Jl Katrawijaya

Bajra Sandhi Monument

Jl Dr Kusumah Atmaja

Jl Panjaitan

Letda Tantular

Jl Raya Puputan

Jl Tukad Gangga

Jl Cok Agung Tresna

Jl Ki Hajar Dewantara

Jl Raya Puputan

Jl Teuku Umar

Jl Serma Mendara

Jl Diponegoro

Jl Diponegoro

Sungai Badung

Jl Surapati

Pura Jagatnatha

Jl Kapten Agung

Jl Sugianyar

Museum Negeri Propinsi Bali

Jl Gajah Mada

Jl Sudirman

Jl Udayana

Jl Teuku Umar

Kube Dharma Bakti

Jl Kartini

Jl Hasanudin

Sungai Badung

Jl Nusakambangan

Jl Imam Bonjol

Jl Thamrin

Sights

Bajra Sandhi Monument

MONUMENT

1 ⊙ MAP P108, E4

The centrepiece to a popular park, this huge monument is as big as its name. Inside the vaguely Borobudur-like structure are dioramas tracing Bali's history. Note that in the portrayal of the 1906 battle with the Dutch, the King of Badung is literally a sitting target. Take the spiral stairs to the top for 360-degree views. (Monument to the Struggle of the People of Bali; ☎0361-264517; Jl Raya Puputan, Renon; adult/child 20,000/10,000Rp; ☺9am-6pm)

Museum Negeri Propinsi Bali

MUSEUM

2 ⊙ MAP P108, C1

Think of this as the British Museum or the Smithsonian of Balinese culture. It's all here, but unlike those world-class institutions, you have to work at sorting it out – the museum could use a dose of curatorial energy. Most displays are labelled in English. The museum comprises several buildings and pavilions, including many examples of Balinese architecture, housing prehistoric pieces, traditional artefacts, Barong (mythical lion-dog creatures), ceremonial objects and rich displays of textiles. (☎0361-222680; Jl Mayor Wisnu; adult/child 50,000/25,000Rp; ☺7.30am-3.30pm Sat-Thu, to 1pm Fri)

Entrance gate, Museum Negeri Propinsi Bali

Pura Jagatnatha   HINDU TEMPLE

3 🎯 MAP P108, C1

The state temple, built in 1953, is dedicated to the supreme god, Sanghyang Widi. Part of its significance is its statement of monotheism. Although the Balinese recognise many gods, the belief in one supreme god (who can have many manifestations) brings Balinese Hinduism into conformity with the first principle of Pancasila – the 'Belief in One God'. (Jl Surapati; admission free)

Kube Dharma Bakti   MASSAGE

4 🎯 MAP P108, C4

Many Balinese wouldn't think of having a massage from anyone but a blind person. Government-sponsored schools offer lengthy courses to certify blind people in reflexology, shiatsu massage, anatomy and much more. In this airy building redolent with liniments you can choose from a range of therapies. (📞0361-749 9440; Jl Serma Mendara 3; massage per hr 100,000Rp; ⏰9am-10pm)

Eating

Depot Cak Asmo   INDONESIAN $

5 🍴 MAP P108, D4

Join the government workers and students from the nearby university for superb dishes cooked to order in the bustling kitchen. Order the buttery and crispy *cumi cumi* (calamari) battered in *telor asin* (a heavenly mixture of eggs and gar-

lic). Fruity ice drinks are a cooling treat. An English-language menu makes ordering a breeze. It's halal, so there's no alcohol. (📞0361-256246; Jl Tukad Gangga; mains from 15,000Rp; ⏰9.30am-11pm)

Warung Lembongan   INDONESIAN $

6 🍴 MAP P108, E3

Silver folding chairs at long tables are shaded by a garish green awning out front. These are details you will quickly forget after you have the house speciality: chicken lightly fried yet delicately crispy like the top of a perfect crème brûlée. The other speciality is a spicy *sop kepala ikan* (fish soup). (📞0361-221437; Jl Cok Agung Tresna 6C; meals 17,000-25,000Rp; ⏰8am-10pm)

Men Gabrug   BALINESE $

7 🍴 MAP P108, E2

A favourite sweet treat for Balinese of all ages is *jaje laklak* – disks of rice flour cooked in an open-air cast-iron pan and redolent of coconut. One of the best places to get them is at this family-run outlet where the cooking takes place right on the street. (📞0361-7070 8415; Jl Drupadi; snacks from 10,000Rp; ⏰9am-6pm Mon-Sat)

Drinking

Bhineka Djaja   COFFEE

8 🎯 MAP P108, B1

Home to Bali's Coffee Co, this storefront sells locally grown

Dining (or Not) Balinese Style

🍽

Eating is a solitary exercise in Bali and conversation is limited. Families rarely eat together; everyone makes up their own plate whenever they're hungry.

The Balinese eat with their right hand, which is used to give and receive all good things. It's customary to wash your hands before eating, even if you use utensils; local restaurants always have a sink outside the restrooms. If you choose to eat the local way, use the bowl of water provided at the table to wash your hands after the meal, as licking your fingers is not appreciated.

Balinese are formal about behaviour and clothing, and it isn't polite to enter a restaurant or eat a meal half-naked, no matter how many sit-ups you've been doing or how many new piercings and tattoos you've acquired.

If you wish to eat in front of a Balinese, it's polite to invite them to join you, even if you know they will say 'no' or you don't have anything to offer. If you're invited to a Balinese home for a meal, your hosts will no doubt insist you eat more, but you may always politely pass on second helpings or refuse food you don't find appealing.

beans and makes a mean espresso, which you can enjoy at the two tiny tables while watching the bustle of Denpasar's old main drag. (📞0361-224016; Jl Gajah Mada 80; coffee 7000Rp; ⏰9am-3pm Mon-Sat)

Shopping

Jepun Bali

TEXTILES

9 🔒 MAP P108, B4

It's like your own private version of the Museum Negeri Propinsi Bali: Gusti Ayu Made Mardiani is locally famous for her *endek* (traditional sarong) and *songket* (silver- or gold-threaded cloth) clothes woven using traditional techniques. You can visit her gracious home and workshop and see the old machines in action, then ponder her beautiful polychromatic selections in silk and cotton. (📞0361-726526; Jl Raya Sesetan, Gang Ikan Mas 11; ⏰call for appointment)

Pasar Badung

MARKET

10 🔒 MAP P108, B1

Busy in the mornings and evenings, Bali's largest food market is a great place to browse and bargain, with food from all over the island, including fruits and spices. (📞0361-224361; Jl Gajah Mada; ⏰24hr)

Explore ⊛
Ubud

Ubud is a place where traditional Balinese culture imbues every waking moment, where colourful offerings adorn the streets and where the hypnotic strains of gamelan are an ever-present soundtrack to everyday life. It's also somewhere that is relentlessly on trend: a showcase of sustainable design, mindfulness, culinary inventiveness and the very best that global tourism has to offer.

The Short List

○ **Ubud's Ricefields (p114)** *Wandering trails and paths through verdant fields on the edge of town.*

○ **Dance Performances (p129)** *Enjoying graceful dance movements and a gamelan orchestra in an evening temple performance.*

○ **Cafe Culture (p127)** *Sipping coffee made with locally grown beans and enjoying ultra-fresh organic meals.*

○ **Cooking Courses (p122)** *Preparing a kick-arse nasi campur at one of the town's many cookery schools.*

○ **Shopping (p14)** *Browsing chic homewares, clothing and handicrafts boutiques.*

Getting There & Around

🚍 The Perama tourist shuttle terminal is located in Padangtegal, south of the town centre. The Kura-Kura bus runs from near Ubud Palace to its hub in Kuta five times daily.

🚗 A taxi or hired car with driver from the airport to Ubud will cost 350,000Rp (400,000Rp between midnight and 6am). A hired car with driver to the airport will cost about the same.

Ubud Map on p118

Dancer near Ubud during a full moon ceremony CHEN WS / SHUTTERSTOCK ©

Top Experience 📷
Explore Ubud's Urban Rice Fields

There's nothing like a walk through the verdant rice fields of Ubud to make things right with the world. These green and ancient terraces spill down lush hillsides to rushing rivers below. Wandering along, you can hear the symphony of frogs, bugs and the constant gurgle of water. Most fields produce three crops a year and even on a short walk you'll see tender shoots, vibrant seas of green and the grain-heavy heads of mature plants.

Walk it Yourself

From the Ibah Luxury Villas driveway, off Jl Raya Campuan in Campuan, take the path to the left, where a walkway crosses the river to the small and serene Pura Gunung Lebah (p121). Follow the concrete path north onto the ridge between the two rivers where you can see the rice fields above Ubud folding over the hills in all directions.

Bali Bird Walks

For keen birdwatchers, this popular **tour** (0361-975009; www.balibirdwalk.com; tour incl lunch US$37; 9am-12.30pm Tue, Fri, Sat & Sun) started by Victor Mason draws flocks. A gentle morning's walk will give you the opportunity to see maybe 30 of the 100 or so local species. The tours leave from the former Beggar's Bush Bar on Jl Raya Campuan.

Bali Nature Herbal Walks

Three-hour **walks** (0812 381 6020, 0812 381 6024; www.baliherbalwalk.com; tour 200,000Rp; 8.30am) traverse lush Bali landscape; medicinal and cooking herbs and plants are identified and explained in their natural environment. Includes herbal drinks.

Banyan Tree Cycling Tours

Day-long **tours** (0813 3879 8516; www.banyantreebiketours.com; tours adult/child from US$55/35) take in remote villages in the hills above Ubud. It's locally owned, and the tours emphasise interaction with villagers. These are very popular and have inspired a bevy of competitors.

Make a Discovery

Parts of Ubud may seem chock-a-block with development but you'd be surprised how often you can find beautiful emerald-green rice fields, just by ducking down a lane. Try this along Jl Bisma or even Monkey Forest Rd.

★ Top Tips

○ Tail a family of local ducks through the rice fields; if a path peters out you can always go back.

○ Bring water, a good hat, decent shoes and wet-weather gear for the afternoon showers.

○ Try to start walks at daybreak, before it gets too hot.

○ Some entrepreneurial rice farmers have erected little toll gates across their fields. You can detour around them or pay a fee (never, ever accede to more than 10,000Rp).

✕ Take a Break

A stroll through the rice fields calls for a snack. **Bali Buda** (Map p118, F5; 0361-976324; www.balibuda.com; Jl Jembawan 1; mains 38,000-67,000Rp, pizzas 63,000-81,000Rp; 7am-10pm;) has an organic market and bakery, where you can choose from a range of tasty treats to stash in your daypack (snacks from 10,000Rp).

Walking Tour

A Perfect Ubud Day

Ubud's centre is as compact as it is colourful, making it a wonderful destination to explore on foot. When here, you'll be spoiled for choice when it comes to eating, drinking and shopping opportunities, and delighted when you sample some of the many rich cultural experiences that the town has to offer.

Walk Facts

Start Museum Puri Lukisan
End Hujon Locale
Length 6km; 1¼ hours

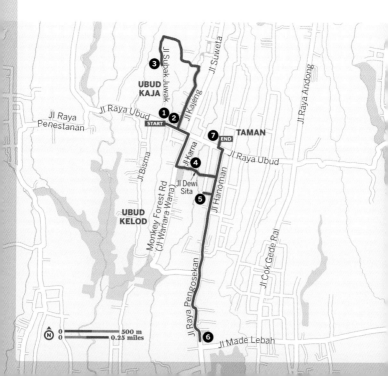

❶ Introduction to Balinese Painting

You're in Bali's artistic heartland, so it's appropriate to start your day getting a good grounding in Balinese art at the **Museum Puri Lukisan** (p120). Set in a well-tended garden, the museum's four buildings are repositories for works by masters including I Gusti Nyoman Lempad and Ida Bagus Made.

❷ Ubud's Water Temple

As well as being an important worship site for locals, **Pura Taman Saraswati** (p121) is one of the prettiest locations in Ubud. Waters from the temple at the rear feed a pond overflowing with photogenic lotus blossoms, and carvings honour Dewi Saraswati, the goddess of wisdom and the arts, who has clearly given her blessing to Ubud.

❸ Rice Fields Detour

It seems extraordinary that bucolic rice fields where local farmers toil can be found just minutes from Ubud's main street, but those who follow the 'Rice Field View' sign from JI Kajeng will soon find that this is the case. Enjoying a drink or simple meal at **Sweet Orange Warung** (p127) in the middle of the fields is a delight.

❹ Browsing Boutiques

You won't find any shortage of shopping opportunities in Ubud, but if you head to Monkey Forest Rd and JI Dewi Sita you'll find that the boutiques there are a cut above the Ubud average. Start with the sweetly-scented **Kou** (p130) and then add to your shopping bag at nearby homewares, clothing and produce shops.

❺ A Spa Interlude

Ubud is known for its spas, yoga schools and health resorts, and **Taksu Spa** (p123) is a place that fits in all three categories. Spend a few hours taking a yoga class, enjoying a massage and relaxing over lunch or a juice in its healthy garden cafe.

❻ Dance Performance

The graceful movements of dancers and melodious sounds of gamelan orchestras make dance performances in Ubud the ultimate entertainment option. Local troops perform at a number of temple compounds around town, and also on the **AMRA open stage** (p130) at the Agung Rai Museum of Art.

❼ Creative Cuisine

It's been an active day, so you're entitled to a relaxing dinner. **Hujon Locale** (p123) is one of Ubud's best restaurants, serving creative and delicious Indonesian fare in casually stylish surrounds. Toast your perfect day with a cocktail, and prepare to enjoy a memorable meal.

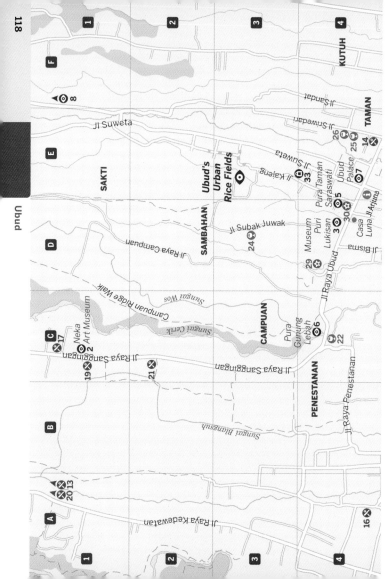

Ubud's Urban Rice Fields

KUTUH

TAMAN

SAKTI

SAMBAHAN

CAMPUAN

PENESTANAN

Neka Art Museum

Campuan Ridge Walk

Jl Suweta

Jl Srwedari

Jl Sandat

Jl Suweta

Jl Kajeng

Jl Raya Campuan

Jl Subak Juwak

Pura Taman Saraswati

Ubud Palace

Puri Lukisan Museum

Casa Luna Jl Arjuna

Jl Bisma

Pura Gunung Lebah

Jl Raya Ubud

Sungai Wos

Sungai Cerik

Jl Raya Sanggingan

Jl Raya Sanggingan

Sungai Blangsuh

Jl Raya Penestanan

Jl Raya Kedewatan

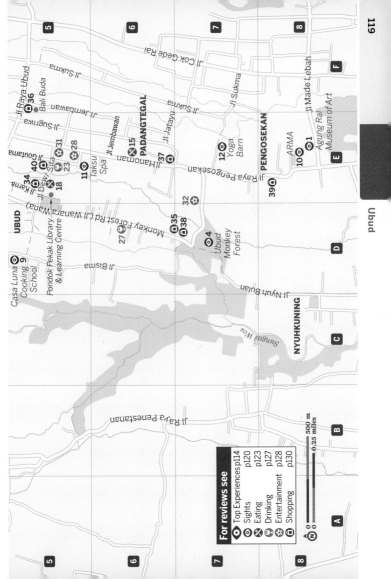

Ubud

For reviews see
◉	Top Experiences	p114
◉	Sights	p120
✕	Eating	p123
◯	Drinking	p127
★	Entertainment	p128
▢	Shopping	p130

500 m
0.25 miles

UBUD

PADANGTEGAL

PENGOSEKAN

NYUHKUNING

Jl Raya Ubud
Jl Sukma
Jl Jembawan
Jl Sugriwa
Jl Goutama
Jl Karna
Jl Dewi Sita
Jl Jembawan
Jl Jatayu
Jl Sukma
Jl Cok Gede Rai
Jl Sukma
Jl Made Lebah
Jl Raya Pengosekan
Jl Bisma
Jl Nyuh Bulan
Jl Raya Penestanan
Monkey Forest Rd (Jl Wanara Wana)
Sungai Wos

Casa Luna ◉ 9
Cooking School
Pondok Pekak Library & Learning Centre

Bali Buda ▢ 36
40 ▢ 34
31 ★
28 ▢
23 ★
Taksu Spa 11 ◉
18 ✕
15 ✕ Hanoman
37 ▢
27 ◉ 35 ▢ 38 ▢
32 ★
◉ 4 Ubud Monkey Forest
12 ◉ Yoga Barn
39 ▢
ARMA
10 ◉ 1 ◉ Agung Rai Museum of Art

Sights

Agung Rai Museum of Art

GALLERY

1 ◉ MAP P118, E8

If you only visit one museum in Ubud, make it this one. Founder Agung Rai built his fortune selling Balinese artwork to foreigners in the 1970s, and during his time as a dealer he also built one of Indonesia's most impressive private collections of art. This cultural compound opened in 1996 and displays his collection in two purpose-built gallery buildings – highlights include the wonderful 19th-century *Portrait of a Javanese Nobleman and his Wife* by Javanese artist Raden Saleh (1807–1880). (ARMA; ☎0361-976659; www.armabali.com/museum; Jl Raya Pengosekan; adult/child under 10yr 100,000Rp/free; ☺9am-6pm)

Neka Art Museum

GALLERY

2 ◉ MAP P118, C1

Offering an excellent introduction to Balinese art, this impressive museum displays its top-notch collection of works in a series of pavilions and halls. Don't miss the multi-room Balinese Painting Hall, which showcases *wayang* (puppet) style as well as the European-influenced Ubud and Batuan styles introduced in the 1920s and 1930s. Also notable is the Lempad Pavilion, with works by the master I Gusti Nyoman Lempad (1862–1978), and the East-West Art Annexe, where works by Affandi (1907–1990) and Widayat (1919–2002) impress. (☎0361-975074; www.museumneka.com; Jl Raya Sanggingan; adult/child under 12yr 75,000Rp/free; ☺9am-5pm)

Museum Puri Lukisan

MUSEUM

3 ◉ MAP P118, D4

It was in Ubud that the modern Balinese art movement started, when artists first began to abandon purely religious themes and court subjects for scenes of everyday life. This museum set in a lovely formal garden has four buildings displaying works from all schools and periods of Balinese art, with a focus on modern masters including I Gusti Nyoman Lempad (1862–1978), Ida Bagus Made (1915–1999) and I Gusti Made Kwandji (1936–2013). All works are labelled in English. (Museum of Fine Arts; ☎0361-975136; www.museumpurilukisan.com; off Jl Raya Ubud; adult/child under 11yr 85,000Rp/free; ☺9am-5pm)

Ubud Monkey Forest

PARK

4 ◉ MAP P118, D7

This cool and dense swath of jungle, officially called Mandala Wisata Wanara Wana, houses three holy temples. The sanctuary is inhabited by a band of more than 600 grey-haired and greedy long-tailed Balinese macaques who are nothing like the innocent-looking doe-eyed monkeys on the brochures – they can bite, so be careful around them. Note that the temples are only open to worshippers. (Mandala Wisata Wanara Wana; ✆0361-971304; www.monkeyforestubud.com; Monkey Forest Rd; adult/child 3-12 years 50,000/40,000Rp; ⏰8.30am-5.30pm)

Pura Taman Saraswati

HINDU TEMPLE

5 ◉ MAP P118, D4

Waters from the temple at the rear of this site feed the pond in the front, which overflows with pretty lotus blossoms. There are carvings that honour Dewi Saraswati, the goddess of wisdom and the arts, whose presence seems to penetrate all of Ubud. Regular dance performances are staged here by night. (Jl Raya Ubud; admission free)

Pura Gunung Lebah

HINDU TEMPLE

6 ◉ MAP P118, C4

This old temple, which sits on a jutting rock at the confluence of two tributaries of Sungai Cerik (*campuan* means 'two rivers'), has recently benefited from a huge building campaign. The setting is magical; listen to the rushing waters while admiring the impressive multi-stepped *meru* (multi-tiered shrine) and a wealth of elaborate carvings. (off Jl Raya Campuan)

Ubud Palace

PALACE

7 ◉ MAP P118, E4

This palace and its temple, **Puri Saren Agung** (cnr Jl Raya Ubud & Jl Suweta; admission free), share a compound in the heart of Ubud.

Pura Taman Saraswati

Massage, Spas & Yoga

Ubud brims with salons and spas where you can heal, pamper, rejuvenate or otherwise focus on your personal needs, physical and mental. Visiting a spa is at the top of many a traveller's itinerary and the business of spas, yoga and other treatments grows each year. Expect the latest trends from any of many practitioners and prepare to try some new therapies. You may also wish to seek out a *balian* (female shaman).

Many spas also offer courses in therapies, treatments and activities such as yoga and massage.

Most of its structures were built after the 1917 earthquake and the local royal family still lives here. You can wander around most of the compound and explore the many traditional, though not excessively ornate, buildings. Though closed for renovation when we last visited, the main pavilion often hosts evening dance performances. (cnr Jl Raya Ubud & Jl Suweta; admission free; ⏰9am-7pm)

Balinese Farm Cooking School
COOKING

8 ◎ MAP P118, F1

Spend a day out in untrammelled countryside 18km north of Ubud *and* learn how to cook Balinese food. This highly recommended cooking course is held in a village and is run by villagers passionate about organic farming. Students learn about local produce and foods; morning courses include a visit to a local produce market. Vegan, vegetarian and omnivore courses available. (☎0812 3953 4446; www.balinesecooking.net; Banjar Patas, Taro; 1-day course adult/child 400,000/250,000Rp)

Casa Luna Cooking School
COOKING

9 ◎ MAP P118, D5

A different cooking class or food tour is offered every day of the week at this well-regarded cooking school associated with the **Casa Luna** (Map p118, D4; ☎0361-977409; www.casalunabali.com; Jl Raya Ubud; mains 50,000-125,000Rp; ⏰8am-11pm; P🛜) restaurant. Half-day courses cover a range of dishes; some include a market visit. A three-hour tour to the famous Gianyar night market is offered on Thursday and Friday, and a 'Food as Medicine' class on Saturday. (☎0361-973282; www.casalunabali.com/casa-luna-cooking-school; Honeymoon Guesthouse, Jl Bisma; classes from 400,000Rp)

ARMA
CULTURAL TOUR

10 ◎ MAP P118, E8

A cultural powerhouse offering classes in painting, woodcarving, gamelan and batik. Other courses include Balinese dance, Hinduism and architecture. (📞0361-976659; www.armabali.com/museum/cultural-workshops; Jl Raya Pengosekan; classes from US$25; 🕐9am-6pm)

Taksu Spa

SPA

11 ◉ MAP P118, E5

One of Ubud's most popular spas, Taksu has a long and rather lavish menu of massages and beauty treatments, as well as a strong focus on yoga. There are private rooms for couples massages and a healthy garden cafe. (📞0361-479 2525; www.taksuspa.com; Jl Goutama; massage from 450,000Rp; 🕐9am-10pm)

Yoga Barn

YOGA

12 ◉ MAP P118, E7

The chakra for the yoga revolution in Ubud, the life force that is the Yoga Barn sits in its own lotus position amid trees near a river valley. The name exactly describes what you'll find: a huge space offering a similarly large range of classes in various yoga practices. There's also an on-site Ayurvedic spa and a garden cafe. (📞0361-971236; www.theyogabarn.com; off Jl Raya Pengosekan; classes from 130,000Rp; 🕐6am-9pm)

Eating

Nasi Ayam Kedewatan

BALINESE $

13 ◉ MAP P118, A1

Few locals making the trek up the hill through Sayan pass this Bali version of a roadhouse without stopping. The star is *sate lilit:* chicken is minced, combined with a selection of spices including lemongrass, then moulded onto bamboo skewers and grilled. It's served as part of the *nasi ayam campur* (25,000Rp) or *nasi ayam pisah* (35,000Rp) set meals. (📞0361-974795; Jl Raya Kedewatan, Kedewatan; mains 25,000-35,000Rp; 🕐8am-6pm)

Hujon Locale

INDONESIAN $$

14 ◉ MAP P118, E4

Chef Will Meyrick is the culinary genius behind Mama San in Seminyak, and his Ubud outpost

---

Refill Your Water Bottle ⚠

The number of plastic water bottles emptied in Bali's tropical heat daily and then tossed in the trash is colossal. In Ubud there are a few places where you can refill your water bottle (plastic or reusable) for a small fee, usually 3000Rp for a large bottle, 2000Rp for a small bottle. The water is the same Aqua brand that is preferred locally and you'll be helping to preserve Bali's beauty, one plastic bottle at a time. A good central location is **Pondok Pekak Library & Learning Centre** (Map p118, E5; 📞0361-976194; www.facebook.com/pg/pondokpekak; off Monkey Forest Rd; 🕐9am-9pm).

is just as impressive. The menu delivers traditional Indonesian with modern, creative flair and the results are uniformly delicious. The setting within a chic colonial-style two-storey bungalow is casually stylish and cleverly flexible – enjoy cocktails and snacks in the downstairs lounge; lunch and dinner upstairs. (📞0813 3972 0306; www.hujanlocale.com; Jl Sriwedari 5; mains 120,000-200,000Rp; ⏰noon-10pm; 🛜🍴)

Kafe
CAFE $$

15 🍴 MAP P118, E6

This is the type of place that Ubud does particularly well. Attractive decor, laid-back vibe, friendly staff and healthy food are the hallmarks, and together they form a tempting package. The huge organic menu has something for most tastes, with a huge range of vegan, veggie and raw offerings with Balinese, Indonesian, Indian and Mexican accents. Good value. (📞0361-479 2078; www.kafe-bali.com; Jl Hanoman 44; sandwiches & wraps 65,000-89,000Rp, mains 39,000-97,000Rp; ⏰7am-11pm; 🛜🍴)

Moksa
VEGETARIAN $$

17 🍴 MAP P118, A4

Based at its own permaculture farm, Moksa shows that extraordinary meals can be created with vegetables prepared simply. Half the dishes are raw, half cooked; many are vegan. The setting is bucolic, but the kitchen is state of the art – a fab mix. The approach is via

a path through fields: follow the signs from Jl Raya Sayan. (📞0813 3977 4787; www.moksaubud.com; Gang Damai, Sayan; mains 40,000-80,000Rp; ⏰10am-8.30pm; 🍴)

Uma Cucina
ITALIAN $$

19 🍴 MAP P118, C1

There's lots to like about this Italian restaurant. Its flexible kitchen serves an antipasto set menu at lunch (eight antipasti, 299,000Rp), a filling afternoon tea (200,000Rp) and dinners featuring pizza cooked in a wood-fired oven, handmade pasta, classic Italian mains and delectable desserts. On Sunday the brunch buffet (from 399,000Rp) with its child-friendly entertainment is particularly popular with families. (📞0361-972448; www.comohotels.com/en/umaubud/dining/uma-cucina; Como Uma Ubud, Jl Raya Sanggingan; pizzas 100,000-180,000Rp, mains 110,000-240,000Rp; ⏰noon-10.30pm Mon-Sat, from 11.30am Sun; 🛜🍴👪)

Pica
SOUTH AMERICAN $$$

20 🍴 MAP P118, E5

Much acclaimed, the contemporary South American cuisine served at this small restaurant is one of Ubud's culinary highlights. From the open kitchen, dishes making creative use of meat and fish issue forth – be sure to ask about daily specials. In our opinion, ordering the delectable tre leche dessert should be mandatory. Bookings advisable.

(☎0361-971660; www.facebook.com/
PicaSouthAmericanKitchen; Jl Dewi
Sita; mains 170,000-330,000Rp; ⏰6-
10pm Tue-Sun; 📶)

Room4Dessert

DESSERTS $$$

21  MAP P118, C1

Celebrity chef Will Goldfarb, who
hails from the States and gained
fame via Netflix's *Chef's Table*, runs
what could be a nightclub but is in
fact a dessert bar where patrons
who book far enough in advance
(you'll need to do so at least a
month before your visit) can enjoy
a decadent nine-course tasting
menu matched with cocktails/
mocktails/wine. (R4D; ☎0821 4429
3452; www.room4dessert.asia; Jl Raya
Sanggingan; tasting dessert & cocktail
menu 1,000,000Rp; ⏰5-11pm Tue-Sun)

Kubu

MEDITERRANEAN $$$

22  MAP P118, A1

Resembling a posh version of the
Balinese bamboo hut that it is
named for, Mandapa's premier
restaurant offers a memorable
and romantic dining experience.
Reserve a table in the main dining
area or opt for a private cabana
overlooking the Sengai (river)
Ayung. Chef Maurizio Bombini's
Mediterranean-European cuisine
is as excellent as the surrounds
and service. Be sure to book well
in advance. (☎0361-4792777; www.
ritzcarlton.com/en/hotels/indonesia/
mandapa/dining; Mandapa Resort,
Jl Kedewatan, Kedewatan; mains
280,000-500,000Rp, degustation
menus 750,000-1,150,000Rp; ⏰6.30-
11pm)

Dishes from Casa Luna Cooking School (p122)

Showing Respect

(i)

Bali has a well-deserved reputation for being mellow, which is all the more reason to respect your hosts, who are enormously forgiving of faux pas if you're making a sincere effort. Be aware and respectful of local sensibilities, and dress and act appropriately, especially in rural villages and at religious sites. When in doubt, let the words 'modest' and 'humble' guide you.

Dos & Don'ts

o You'll see shorts and short skirts everywhere on locals but overly revealing clothing is still frowned upon, as is wandering down the street shirtless quaffing a beer.

o Many women go topless on Bali's beaches, offending locals who are embarrassed by foreigners' gratuitous nudity.

o Don't touch anyone on the head; it's regarded as the abode of the soul and is therefore sacred.

o Do pass things with your right hand. Even better, use both hands. Just don't use only your left hand, as it's considered unclean.

o Beware of talking with hands on hips – a sign of contempt, anger or aggression (as displayed in traditional dance and opera).

o Beckon someone with the hand extended and using a downward waving motion. The Western method of beckoning is considered very rude.

o Don't make promises of gifts, books and photographs that are soon forgotten. Think of the hopeful local checking their mailbox or email inbox every day.

o Cover shoulders and knees if visiting a temple or mosque; in Bali, a *selandang* (traditional scarf) or sash plus a sarong is usually provided for a small donation or as part of the entrance fee.

o Women are asked not to enter temples if they're menstruating, pregnant or have recently given birth. At these times women are thought to be *sebel* (ritually unclean).

o Don't put yourself higher than a priest, particularly at festivals (eg by scaling a wall to take photos).

o Take off your shoes before entering a mosque.

Mozaic
FUSION $$$

23 ✗ MAP P118, C2

Chef Chris Salans oversees this much-lauded top-end restaurant. Fine French fusion cuisine features on a constantly changing seasonal menu that takes its influences from tropical Asia. Dine in an elegant garden twinkling with romantic lights or within an ornate pavilion. Tasting menus are obligatory, unless you wish to limit yourself to tapas in the lounge (from 5pm). Lunch is available during high season only. (📞0361-975768; www.mozaic-bali.com; Jl Raya Sanggingan; lunch tasting menu 500,000-700,000Rp, dinner tasting menu 700,000-1,600,000Rp; ⏱6-9.45pm Mon-Wed, noon-2pm & 6-9.45pm Thu-Sun; 📶📡)

Drinking

Bridges
LOUNGE

25 🍺 MAP P118, C4

The namesake bridges are right outside the Divine Wine & Cocktail Bar on the lower level of this bar/restaurant complex, which has sweeping views of the river gorge. You'll hear the rush of the water far below while you indulge in a top-end cocktail. There are gourmet bites for sharing and a long wine list for exploring. (📞0361-970095; www.bridgesbali.com; Jl Raya Campuan, Bridges Bali; ⏱4-11.30pm daily, happy hour 4-6.30pm Sat-Thu)

Night Rooster
COCKTAIL BAR

26 🍺 MAP P118, E5

From the same folks at **Locavore** (📞0361-977733; www.restaurant locavore.com; Jl Dewi Sita; 5-course menu 675,000-775,000Rp, 7-course menu 775,000-875,000Rp; ⏱6.30-9pm Mon, noon-2pm & 6.30-9pm Tue-Sat; 🅿❄📶), this neighbouring, second-storey cocktail bar boasts a talented mixologist and some fascinating flavour combos. Inventive cocktails include things such as jackfruit-infused dry gin, homemade bitters and flaming cassia bark.

The selection of appetisers and cheese and charcuterie platters make for satisfying pairings. (📞0361-977733; www.locavore.co.id/nightrooster; Jl Dewi Sita 10B; ⏱4pm-midnight Mon-Sat)

Sweet Orange Warung
CAFE

27 🍺 MAP P118, D3

An idyllic location in the midst of a rice field a short walk from the centre of town makes this a wonderful spot for a drink or simple meal. You'll be serenaded by water running through the farming channels, birds singing and local children playing.

Drinks include French-press coffee, beer and fresh juice. (📞0813 3877 8689; www.sweet-orangewarung.com; Jl Subak Juwak; ⏱9am-8.30pm)

Coffee Studio Seniman
CAFE

28 [icon] MAP P118, E4

That 'coffee studio' moniker isn't for show; the baristas here make a point of experimenting with different styles of single-origin coffee. Take a seat on the designer rocker chairs and choose from a menu of pourovers, syphon, cold brew, Aeropress or espresso using house-roasted Indonesian beans. It's also popular for food (mains 43,000Rp to 111,000Rp). ([phone]0361-972085; www.senimancoffee.com; Jl Sriwedari 5; [time]8am-10pm; [wifi])

Seniman Spirits
BAR

29 [icon] MAP P118, E4

The caffeinated masterminds behind the Seniman coffee brand recently opened this bar next to their coffee studio, and it has become one of Ubud's most fashionable drinking dens. Espresso martinis are the cocktail of choice. (Bar Seniman; www.senimancoffee.com; Jl Sriwedari; [time]6pm-midnight)

No Màs
BAR

30 [icon] MAP P118, D6

DJs and Latin bands crank the volume up every night at this small bar on one of the town's main strips, and there are occasional theme nights too. It can get hot when the dancing starts, but the pool bar in the rear garden provides a welcome relief. ([phone]0361-9080800; www.nomasubud.com; Monkey Forest Rd; [time]5pm-1am)

Entertainment

Paradiso
CINEMA

31 [star] MAP P118, E5

Sharing a building with the vegan **Earth Cafe & Market** ([phone]0361-976546; www.earthcafebali.com; mains 79,000-98,000Rp; [time]7am-10pm; [wifi][icon]), this surprisingly plush 150-seat cinema screens two films daily. The price of admission is redeemable against items from the cafe menu – so a great deal. Monday are half-price; on Tuesday and Thursday a community choir sings here. Check the website for a schedule. ([phone]0361-976546; www.paradisoubud.com; Jl Gautama Selatan; incl food or drinks 50,000Rp; [time]films from 5pm)

Pura Dalem Ubud
DANCE

32 [star] MAP P118, D4

This open-air venue in a temple compound has a flame-lit carved-stone backdrop and is an evocative place to see a dance performance. Different companies perform Legong (7.30pm Tuesday and Saturday), Jegog (7.30pm Wednesday), Barong (7pm Thursday) and the Kecak fire dance (7.30pm Monday and Friday). (Jl Raya Ubud; adult/child under 10yr 80,000/40,000Rp; [time]Mon-Sat)

Pura Taman Saraswati
DANCE

33 [star] MAP P118, D4

The beauty of the setting may distract you from the dancers,

The Magic of Dance

Few travel experiences are more magical than watching Balinese dance, especially in Ubud and the surrounding villages. You can see Kecak, Legong and Barong dances, Mahabharata and Ramayana ballets, *wayang kulit* (shadow-puppet plays) and gamelan (traditional Javanese and Balinese orchestras).

Dances performed for visitors are usually adapted and abbreviated to some extent to make them more enjoyable, but usually have appreciative locals in the audience (or peering around the screen!). It's also common to combine the features of more than one traditional dance in a single performance. The website Ubud Now & Then (www.ubudnowandthen.com) has schedules of special events and performances. Also check with the Fabulous Ubud Tourist Information Centre (p130).

The Best of the Dance Troupes

All dance groups on Ubud's stages are not created equal. There are several excellent troupes who regularly perform in Ubud, including the following.

Semara Ratih High-energy, creative Legong interpretations. The best local troupe musically.

Gunung Sari Legong dance; one of Bali's oldest and most respected troupes.

Semara Madya Kecak dance; especially good for the hypnotic chants. A mystical experience for some.

Tirta Sari Legong dance.

Cudamani One of Bali's best gamelan troupes. It rehearses in Pengosekan, runs a school for children and tours internationally. You have to seek them out, though, as they no longer perform in tourist venues.

although at night you can't see the lily pads and lotus flowers that are such an attraction by day. Janger dance is performed on Sunday and Monday, the Ramayana ballet on Wednesdays and Legong on Saturday. On Tuesday and Thursday, women play the gamelan and children dance. (Ubud Water Palace; Jl Raya Ubud; 80,000Rp; 7.30pm)

Padang Tegal Kaja

DANCE

34 ⭐ MAP P118, E5

A simple, open terrace in a convenient location. In many ways this location hints at what dance performances have looked like in Ubud for generations. Enjoy the Kecak fire dance on Saturday and Sunday or Barong and Keris on Tuesdays. (Jl Hanoman; 75,000Rp; ⏰7.30pm)

ARMA Open Stage

DANCE

Part of the ARMA cultural compound (see 10 Map p118), Open Stage hosts some of the best troupes performing Barong and Legong dance. Performances are held on Tuesday and Sunday at 7.30pm, Wednesday at 7pm and Friday at 6pm. On nights when there is a new or full moon, the Cak Rina trance and fire dance is held at 7.30pm. (☎0361-976659; info@armabali.com; Jl Raya Pengosekan; dance performances 80,000-100,000Rp)

Pondok Bamboo Music Shop

PUPPET THEATRE

35 ⭐ MAP P118, E7

Short shadow-puppet shows are performed here by noted experts. (☎0361-974807; Monkey Forest Rd; tickets 75,000Rp; ⏰performances 8pm Mon & Thu)

Shopping

Threads of Life Indonesian Textile Arts Center

TEXTILES

36 🔒 MAP P118, E4

This textile gallery and shop sponsors the production of naturally dyed, handmade ritual textiles from around Indonesia. It exists to help recover skills in danger of being lost to modern dyeing and weaving methods. Commissioned pieces are displayed in the gallery, which has good explanatory material, and other textiles are available for purchase.

Threads of Life aAlso runs regular **courses** (2-hr class 200,000-400,000Rp; ⏰10am-7pm) on textile appreciation. (☎0361-972187; www.threadsoflife.com; Jl Kajeng 24; ⏰10am-7pm)

Kou

COSMETICS

37 🔒 MAP P118, E5

Concocted from pure coconut oil, the handmade soaps sold here

Tourist Information

ⓘ

The **Fabulous Ubud Tourist Information Centre** (Map p118, E4; ☎0361-973285; www.fabulousubud.com; Jl Raya Ubud; ⏰8am-9pm; 📶) is run by the Ubud royal family and is the one really useful tourist office in Ubud. It offers up-to-date information on events, ceremonies and traditional dances held in the area; dance tickets and tours are sold here.

Dancers perform at an Ubud temple

will bring the evocative scents of frangipani, tuberose, jasmine, orange and lemon tea-tree to your bathroom. The attractive packaging makes their products eminently suitable for gifts.

The proprietors also operate Kou Cuisine. (☎0361-971905, 0821 4556 9663; www.facebook.com/ koubali.naturalsoap; Jl Dewi Sita; ⊙9am-8pm)

Neka Art Museum Shop   BOOKS, SOUVENIRS

One of the best places in Ubud to source top-quality traditional Balinese handicrafts is at the Neka Art Museum (see 2 ◉ Map p118). Also stocks books. (☎0361-975074; www. museumneka.com; Jl Raya Sanggingan; ⊙9am-5pm)

BaliZen   TEXTILES

38 🔒 MAP P118, D6

Locally made cushions, bed and home linens, kimonos and kids clothing are sold at this stylish boutique, all made with fabrics featuring designs drawn from nature or traditional Balinese motifs. Also natural bath products and traditional Balinese umbrellas. (☎0361-976022; www.tokobalizen. com; Monkey Forest Rd; ⊙9am-8pm)

Ganesha Bookshop   BOOKS

39 🔒 MAP P118, F5

Bookshop with a selection of titles on Indonesian-related subjects as well as a large selection of used books, with a particular focus on crime fiction. Also operates as a (charged) book exchange. (📞0361-970320; www.ganeshabooksbali.com; Jl Raya Ubud; 🕘9am-6pm)

Namaste
GIFTS & SOUVENIRS

40 🔒 MAP P118, E6

Just the place to buy a crystal to get your spiritual house in order, Namaste stocks a top range of New Age supplies. Incense, yoga mats, moody instrumental music – it's all here. (📞0361-970528; www.facebook.com/namastethespiritualshop; Jl Hanoman 64; 🕘9am-7pm)

Pondok Bamboo Music Shop
MUSICAL INSTRUMENTS

Hear the music of a thousand bamboo wind chimes at this store

(see 35 ⭐ Map p118) owned by noted gamelan musician Nyoman Warsa, who also offers music lessons. (📞0361-974807; Monkey Forest Rd; music classes per hour 150,000Rp-200,000Rp 🕘9am-8pm)

Utama Spice
COSMETICS

43 🔒 MAP P118, D7

The scent of Utama's Balinese-made natural skincare products wafts out into the street, luring shoppers inside to investigate the pricey but nice essential oils, cosmetics and toiletries sold here. All are made without parabens, mineral oils, synthetic fragrances and artificial colourants. (📞0361-975051; www.utamaspicebali.com; Monkey Forest Rd; 🕘9am-8.30pm)

Neka Art Museum (p120)

IMAGENTLE / SHUTTERSTOCK ©

Goddess on the Go!

CLOTHING

44 🔒 MAP P118, E8

A large selection of women's clothes designed for adventure, made to be super-comfortable, easy to pack and ecofriendly. (☏0361-976084; www.goddessonthego.net; Jl Raya Pengosekan; ⏲9am-5pm)

Confiture de Bali

FOOD

45 🔒 MAP P118, E5

Jams made from local fruits, butters (cashew, lemon and peanut) and kombucha are sold at this sweet boutique. (☏0852 3884 1684; www.confituredebali.net; Jl Goutama 26; ⏲9am-10pm)

Explore

East Bali

Exploring east Bali is one of the island's great pleasures. Rice terraces spill down hillsides, wild volcanic beaches are pounded by surf and traditional villages are barely touched by modernity. Watching over this region is Gunung Agung, the 3142m active volcano known as the 'navel of the world' and 'Mother Mountain'.

The Short List

○ **Pura Lempuyang (p137)** *Visiting important temples and marvelling at panoramic views on a magical uphill trek.*

○ **Sidemen (p140)** *Trekking through green rice fields in this picture-perfect river valley.*

○ **Village Life (p140)** *Chilling out in some of the villages along, and inland of, the beautiful eastern coast.*

○ **Tulamben (p140)** *Diving into the blue waters to explore a shipwreck right off the beach.*

○ **Gianyar Night Market (p139)** *Sampling aromatic and tasty local specialities at one of Bali's best night markets.*

Getting There & Around

🚗 You'll want your own wheels. The coastal highway links most places of interest in east Bali.

🚌 Tourist bus services run to/from south Bali, the port town of Padangbai and the tourist enclave of Candidasa.

East Bali Map on p136

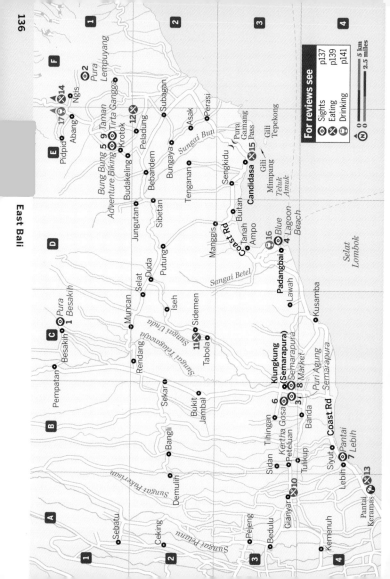

For reviews see

◎ Sights	p137
✕ Eating	p139
◉ Drinking	p141

0 — 5 km
0 — 2.5 miles

Sights

Pura Besakih

HINDU TEMPLE

1 MAP P136, C1

Perched nearly 1000m up the side of Gunung Agung, this is Bali's most important Hindu temple. The site encompasses 23 separate but related temples, with the largest and most important being Pura Penataran Agung, built on six levels terraced up the slope. It has an imposing *candi bentar* (split gateway); note that tourists are not allowed inside. The Pura Besakih complex hosts frequent ceremonies, but the recent eruptions of the volcano have kept both worshipper and visitor numbers down. (60,000Rp, parking 5000Rp)

Pura Lempuyang

HINDU TEMPLE

2 MAP P136, F1

One of the holiest temple complexes on the island (it and Pura Besakih are the most important in east Bali), this group of seven temples has a spectacular setting on the steep slope of Gunung Lempuyang, 10km northeast of Tirta Gangga. (Gunung Lempuyang; donation requested, car/scooter parking 2000Rp/free; ⊘24hr)

Puri Agung Semarapura

PALACE

3 MAP P136, B3

Built when the Dewa Agung dynasty moved here in 1710, this palace compound was laid out as a large square, believed to be in the form of a mandala, with

Pura Besakih

courtyards, gardens, pavilions and moats. Most of the original palace and grounds were destroyed by the 1908 Dutch attacks; all that remain are the carved Pemedal Agung, the gateway on the south side of the square, the **Bale Kambang** (Floating Pavilion; admission incl in palace ticket) and the Kertha Gosa. (Klungkung Palace; Jl Untung Surapati; adult/child 12,000/6000Rp; ☺8am-6pm)

Blue Lagoon Beach BEACH

4 ◉ MAP P136, D3

On the far side of Padangbai's eastern headland, about a 500m walk from the town centre, is this small sandy beach. It has a couple of warungs and gentle, family-friendly surf.

Taman Tirta Gangga GARDENS

5 ◉ MAP P136, E1

This 1.2ha water palace serves as a fascinating reminder of the old Bali. Built for the last Raja of Karangasem in 1946, it was almost fully destroyed by the eruption of nearby Mount Agung in 1963, but has subsequently been rebuilt. Admire the 11-tiered *Nawa Sanga* fountain and the ponds filled with huge koi and lotus blossoms, and jump between the round stepping stones in the water. It's also possible to take a swim in the huge stone spring-water pool. (www.tirtagangga.nl; Jl Abang-Amplapura; adult/child 30,000/15,000Rp, swimming 5000Rp, parking car/scooter 5000/1000Rp; ☺7am-7pm)

Kertha Gosa HISTORIC BUILDING

6 ◉ MAP P136, B3

This open-sided pavilion in the northeastern corner of the Puri Agung Semarapura was effectively the supreme court of the Klungkung kingdom, where disputes and cases that could not be settled at village level were eventually brought. A superb example of Klungkung architecture, it features a ceiling covered with fine 20th-century paintings in Kamasan (aka Wayang) style. These replaced the original 19th-century cloth paintings, which had deteriorated over time, and depict the Garuda story among other scenes. (Hall of Justice; Jl Untung Surapati, Puri Agung Semarapura; admission incl in palace ticket; ☺8am-6pm)

Taman Tirta Gangga

MICHELE FALZONE / GETTY IMAGES ©

Pantai Lebih
BEACH

7 🞉 MAP P136, B4

Just off the coastal highway, Lebih Beach has glittering mica-infused sand. Fishing boats line the shore and the air is redolent with the smell of BBQ fish emanating from a strip of beachside warungs; this is an excellent stop for lunch.

Semarapura Market
MARKET

8 🞉 MAP P136, B3

Klunkgkung's market is a vibrant hub of commerce and a meeting place for people of the region. You can easily spend an hour wandering about the warren of stalls on three levels, and in the surrounding streets. It's grimy, yes, but also fascinating. Huge straw baskets of fresh produce are islands of colour amid the chaos, and there's plenty of jewellery and ikat (the latter sells for a fraction of what you'll pay elsewhere). It's best visited in the morning. (cnr Jl Diponegoro & Jl Puputan; ⏱6am-5pm)

Bung Bung Adventure Biking
CYCLING

9 🞉 MAP P136, E1

Ride downhill through the picture-perfect rice fields, terraces and river valleys around Tirta Gangga with this grassroots tour company. The price includes a guide and use of a mountain bike and helmet. The office is at Homestay Rijasa, across from the Taman Tirta Gangga entrance. Book in advance. (☎0363-21873, 0813 3840 2132; bungbungbikeadventure@gmail.com; Homestay Rijasa, Jl Abang-Amlapura; 2hr-tour 300,000Rp)

Eating

Gianyar Night Market
MARKET $

10 🞉 MAP P136, A3

The sound of scores of cooking pots and the glare of bright lights add a frenetic and festive clamour to Gianyar's delicious and wonderfully aromatic *pasar malam* (night market), where some of the best street food in Bali is on offer. Dozens of stalls set up each night in the town's main street and cook up a mouthwatering and jaw-dropping range of dishes, including delectable *babi guling* (spit-roast pig stuffed with chilli, turmeric, garlic and ginger). (Pasar Senggol Gianyar; Jl Ngurah Rai; dishes from 15,000Rp; ⏱5-11pm)

Dapur Kapulaga
BALINESE $

11 🞉 MAP P136, C2

Serving a predominantly organic menu of Western and Balinese staples, this friendly and clean warung with its distinctive checkerboard-tiled floor is a great choice. You'll find it in front of the Alamdhari Resort & Spa. No alcohol, but the house-concocted Sidemen Cooler steps into the breach nicely. (☎0852 3861 5775; Jl Raya Tebola; mains 32,000-50,000Rp; ⏱1-10pm; 🍴)

Villages of East Bali

Padangbai

This little beach town is the port for public ferries connecting Bali with Lombok and Nusa Penida; there are also fast boats to Lombok and the Gilis. When not inundated by travellers in transit, it has a laid-back vibe and its accommodation, eating and drinking choices are solidly geared towards the backpacker and diving markets.

Tulamben

Tulamben's big attraction sunk over 60 years ago. The wreck of the US cargo ship *Liberty* is among the best and most popular dive sites in Bali and has transformed what was a tiny fishing village into an entire town based on diving. Even snorkellers can easily swim out and enjoy exploring the wreck and the coral reefs that are strung along the coastline.

Sidemen

In Sidemen (pronounced Si-da-men), a walk in any direction is a communion with nature. Winding through one of Bali's most beautiful river valleys, the road to this hilltop village offers marvellous paddy-field scenery, a delightful rural character and extraordinary views of Gunung Agung (when the clouds permit).

Bali Asli

BALINESE $$

12 🍴 MAP P136, E2

The green hills around Amlapura are some of east Bali's most beautiful and Australian chef Penelope Williams takes full advantage of the vistas at her elegant restaurant and cooking school. Produce sourced from the restaurant's own garden is used for meals that explore the vibrancy of Balinese and Indonesian flavours. This may be the best *nasi campur* you'll ever eat. (📱0822 3690 9215; www.baliasli.com.au; Jl Raya Gelumpang, Gelumpang; nasi campur 165,000-228,000Rp; ⏰10am-3pm; 🛜)

Hotel Komune Beach Club

INTERNATIONAL $$

13 🍴 MAP P136, A4

Enjoying the restaurant, bar, pool and outdoor cinema at Hotel Komune's beach club isn't limited to the resort's in-house guests, which is good news for those travelling along the coastal highway in east Bali. The menu includes something for every taste, with burgers, sandwiches, pizza, pasta and Indonesian dishes on offer. We applaud the dedicated vegan and kids menus. (📱0361-301 8888; www.komuneresorts.com/keramasbali/beach-club; sandwiches

& burgers 65,000-95,000Rp; mains 58,000-250,000Rp; ⏱6.30am-11pm; 🛜 ✏ 👪)

Warung Enak

BALINESE $$

14 ✖ MAP P136, F1

Owners Komang and Wayan have their own organic vegetable garden, and use the produce in the tasty dishes created in their busy kitchen. Balinese dishes include a tasty *ikan kare* (fish curry), satays and gado-gado; Western alternatives include pizzas and pastas. Black rice pudding is a popular finale. Drinks include juices, beer and wine by both the glass and bottle. (📞0819 1567 9019; Jl I Ketut Natih, Amed Village; mains 55,000-80,000Rp; ⏱7am-10.30pm; 🛜 ✏)

Vincent's

INTERNATIONAL $$

15 ✖ MAP P136, E3

One of east Bali's better restaurants, Vincent's has several distinct open-air rooms and a large rear garden. The comfy front bar area hosts live jazz on both Monday (high season only) and Thursday (all year), kicking off around 7pm. The menu offers sandwiches, salads, Balinese staples and various Western dishes – the 'coconut texture' dessert is justly popular.

(📞0363-41368; www.vincentsbali. com; Jl Raya Candidasa; mains 75,000-295,000Rp; ⏱11am-10pm; 🛜 ✏)

Drinking

Omang Omang

BAR

16 🍷 MAP P136, D3

A loyal crew of Omangsters (regulars) join a constant stream of blow-ins at this friendly eatery, bar and live-music venue. Nosh on toasties, tacos, burgers and Indonesian favourites, down an ice-cold Bintang or two and rock along with the house blues band on Monday nights. Decent coffee, too. (📞0363-438 1251; www. facebook.com/OmangOmang999; Jl Silayukti 12)

Wawa-Wewe I

BAR

17 🍷 MAP P136, E1

You won't know your wawas from your wewes if you spend an evening downing Bintangs here. This old-fashioned backpackers dive is the coast's most raucous bar – which by local standards means that sometimes it gets sorta loud. Local bands jam from 8pm on Wednesday, Friday and Sunday nights. (📞0812 3973 7662; Lipah; ⏱10am-11pm; 🛜)

Worth a Trip 🔭
Party till Dawn on Gili Trawangan

Gili Trawangan is a tropical playground of global renown. Its heaving main drag – a string of bars, restaurants, shops and guesthouses – can surprise those expecting a languid island retreat. Yet behind this glitzy facade, a bohemian character endures, with rickety warungs and reggae joints surviving between the cocktail tables, and quiet retreats dotting the much-less-busy north coast.

Getting There

🚤 various departure points on Bali (45 minutes to 2½ hours) including Sanur, Benoa Harbour & Padangbai. Fares and times vary; see **Gili Bookings** (www.gilibookings.com) for more.

Beaches

Gili T is ringed by the sort of powdery white sand people expect to find on Bali, but don't. It can be crowded along the bar-lined main part of the strip, but walk just a bit north or south and west and you'll find some of Gili T's nicest swimming and snorkelling beaches. You can discover more solitude in parts of the west and north coasts, where it will be you and your towel on the sand – although water and Bintang vendors are never far away.

Diving & Snorkelling

Trawangan is a diving hot spot, with many professional scuba and freediving schools. Most dive schools and shops have good accommodation packages. Safety standards are reasonably high, but with the proliferation of new dive schools on Gili T, several have formed the Gili Island Divers Association (GIDA). We highly recommend diving with GIDA-associated shops, which come together for monthly meetings on conservation and dive-impact issues.

There's fun snorkelling off the beach 200m north of the boat landing – the coral isn't in the best shape here, but there are tons of fish and turtles. The reef is in slightly better shape off the northwest coast, but at low tide you'll have to scramble over some sharp dead coral (bring rubber booties) to access it.

Nightlife

Gili T has oodles of beachside drinking dens, ranging from sleek lounge bars to simple shacks. Parties are held several nights a week, shifting between mainstay bars such as **Tir na Nog** (☎0370-613 9463; www.tirnanogbar.com; Jl Raya Trawangan; ☻7am-2am Thu-Tue, to 3am Wed; 🛜) and various other upstarts. The strip south of the pier is the centre for raucous nightlife, with places that were once bars now rapidly evolving into full-fledged clubs.

★ **Top Tips**

○ Trawangan is great on foot or by bike. You can walk around the whole island in a couple of hours – if you finish at the hill on the southwestern corner, you'll have terrific sunset views of Bali's Gunung Agung.

○ Note that at low tide large portions of the west and north coasts have rocks and coral near the surface, which makes trying to get off the shore deeply unpleasant.

✕ **Take a Break**

Gili T has slick coffee shops, creative Indo fusion eateries and plenty of healthy cafes. In the evenings numerous places on the main strip grill delicious fresh seafood. The best traditional warung on Gili T, **Warung Dewi** (☎0819 0763 3826; Jl Kardinal; mains 25,000-35,000Rp; ☻7am-8pm), is just a few steps back from the high-priced bustle of the main strip.

Survival Guide

Traditional Barong (p129) mask TROPICAL STUDIO / SHUTTERSTOCK ©

Before You Go

Book Your Stay

Bali has a huge range of great-value accommodation for any budget. If visiting in the peak periods of August and Christmas, book three or more months ahead.

Homestays & Guesthouses Bali's family-run accommodation is comfortable and puts you right in the middle of fascinating local life.

Hotels Many of Bali's hundreds of hotels are located near the action and offer good deals.

Resorts Bali has some of the world's best resorts at prices that would be a bargain elsewhere. You can be on the beach or nestled in a lush mountain valley.

Villas Enjoy a sybaritic escape and private pool.

Useful Websites

Websites such as homeaway.com and airbnb.com have hundreds of listings for Bali villas and private

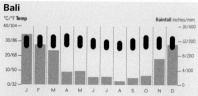

When to Go

High Season (Jul, Aug & Dec) High season is Bali's busiest time. Book ahead for rooms.

Shoulder (May, Jun & Sep) Often the best weather: it's slightly cooler and drier; less crowded.

Low Season (Jan–Apr, Oct & Nov) Low season makes spontaneous travel easy. Things go quiet for the Nyepi holiday.

accommodation. However, many listed properties are not licensed.

Bali Discovery ☎ 0361-286283; www.balidiscovery.com) The main local source for hotel deals (compare their rates to the major websites); also books villas.

Best Budget

Hotel Ayu Lili Garden (☎ 0361-750557) Family-run hotel with high standards and vintage bungalow-style rooms.

M Boutique Hostel (www.mboutiquehostel.com) Contemporary capsule dorms, plus a lovely lawn and small plunge pool.

Three Win Homestay (www.threewinhomestay.com) Modern rooms with comfy beds and spacious bathrooms in a family compound.

Pondok Batur Indah ☎ 0363-22342) Homestay with clean, simple rooms and jaw-dropping rice-terrace views.

Best Midrange

Puri Damai (www.puridamai.com) Elegant apartment-style guesthouse tucked away near Double Six Beach.

Temple Lodge (www.thetemplelodge.com) Creative huts and cottages made from thatch, driftwood and other natural materials, on cliffs overlooking surf breaks.

Maison Aurelia Sanur
(http://preferencehotels.com/maison-aurelia) High-style hotel rooms with plush furnishings and a richly restful decor.

Pemedal Beach (www.pemedalbeach.com) Lovely affordable bungalows near a sandy beach, with an infinity pool.

Swasti Eco Cottages
(www.baliswasti.com) Large compound featuring an organic garden, pool, spa and yoga; a short walk to the Monkey Forest.

Melasti Beach Bungalows (www.melastibeachamed.com) Good-value B&B operated by a genial and welcoming American expat.

Best Top End

Oberoi (www.oberoihotels.com) Balinese-style beachside retreat with luxuries like private verandahs and pools.

Mandapa (www.ritzcarlton.com) Suites and villas set in a spectacular river valley enclosed by rice fields.

Alila Villas Uluwatu
(www.alilahotels.com/uluwatu) Vast and visually stunning resort with an contemporary style.

Hotel Komune (www.komuneresorts.com) Beachfront resort with great surf, plus activities like guided meditation and a kids club with a skate park.

Arriving in Bali

Ngurah Rai International Airport A taxi to Kuta is 80,000Rp, to Seminyak it's 130,000Rp and to Ubud it's 300,000Rp.

Benoa Harbour Pelni ships dock here.

Gilimanuk Ferry service to and from Java.

Sanur Boats to Nusa Lembongan, Nusa Ceningan and Nusa Penida.

Padangbai Boat service to Lombok and the Gili Islands.

Getting Around

Bicycle

o Increasingly, people are touring the island by *sepeda* (bike) and many visitors are using bikes around towns and for day trips.

o There are plenty of bicycles for rent in tourist areas, but many are in poor condition. Ask at your accommodation. Prices are from 30,000Rp per day.

Car & Driver

o An excellent way to travel around Bali is by hired vehicle, allowing you to avoid the driving and inherent frustrations. If you're part of a group, it can make economic sense too.

o It's easy to arrange a charter: just listen for one of the frequent offers of 'transport?' in in tourist centres. Approach a driver or ask at your hotel, which is often a good method as it increases accountability.

o Costs for a full day should average 500,000 Rp to 800,000Rp.

o On the road, buy the driver lunch (they'll want to eat elsewhere, so give them 20,000Rp) and offer snacks and drinks.

Car & Motorbike

o Renting a car or motorbike can open up Bali for

exploration – and can also leave you counting the minutes until you return it; there can be harrowing driving conditions on the islands at certain times and south Bali traffic is often awful. But it gives you the freedom to explore myriad back roads and lets you set your own schedule.

○ Any place you stay will be able to help you organise motorbike rental. Rates are around 60,000Rp per day.

Taxi

○ Metered taxis are common in south Bali and Denpasar (but not Ubud). They are essential for getting around and you can usually flag one down in busy areas. They're often a lot less hassle than haggling with drivers offering 'transport!'

○ The best taxi company by far is **Blue Bird Taxi** (☏0361-701111; www.bluebirdgroup.com), which uses blue vehicles with a light on the roof bearing a stylised bluebird. Drivers speak reasonable English and use the meter at all times. Many expats will use no other firm. Blue Bird has a slick

app that summons a taxi to your location just like Uber. Watch out for fakes – look for 'Blue Bird' over the windscreen and the phone number.

Tourist Shuttle Bus

○ Tourist buses such as **Kura-Kura Bus** (Map p38, F7; ☏0361-757070; www.kura2bus.com; Jl Ngurah Rai Bypass, ground fl, DFS Galleria, Kuta; rides 20,000-80,000Rp, 3-/7-day pass from 150,000/250,000Rp; 📶) and **Perama** (☏0361-751170; www.peramatour.com) are economical and convenient ways to get around. You'll see signs in major tourist areas. Typically a tourist bus is an eight- to 20-passenger vehicle. Service is not as quick as with your own car and driver but it's far easier than trying for public bemos (minibuses) and buses.

Essential Information

Accessible Travel

Sanur and Nusa Dua – where the higher-end

hotels and resorts are located – are more wheelchair-accessible than Kuta, Legian and Seminyak, although there are accessible beach walks in all of these locations. Expect high kerbs, few kerb cuts, badly maintained and crowded pavements, and steps into many establishments. Most temples are only partially wheelchair-accessible at best, stairs being an integral philosophical part of every Hindu temple. However, there is often a way around these stairs – ask a caretaker.

Bali One Care (balionecare.com/en) Can arrange accessible transport and supplies a wide range of mobility and medical equipment, as well as care, nursing and even babysitting services.

Bali Beach Wheels (☏877-6508-5812; balibeachwheels.com) This brand-new company has three Hippocampe beach/all-terrain wheelchairs for hire by the day, week or month for easier access to the beach and rice paddies.

Download Lonely Planet's free Accessible Travel guides from http://lptravel.to/AccessibleTravel.

Business Hours

Banks 8am to 2pm Monday to Thursday, 8am to noon Friday, 8am to 11am Saturday

Government offices 8am to 3pm Monday to Thursday, 8am to noon Friday (although these are not standardised)

Post offices 8am to 2pm Monday to Friday, longer in tourist centres

Restaurants and cafes 8am to 10pm daily

Shops & services 9am to 8pm or later daily

Electricity

Type C
230V/50Hz

Type F
230V/50Hz

Dos & Don'ts

Indonesia is pretty relaxed, but there are a few rules of etiquette.

Body language Use both hands when handing somebody something. Don't show public displays of affection or talk with your hands on your hips (it's seen as aggressive).

Clothing Avoid showing a lot of skin, although many local men wear shorts. Don't go topless if you're a woman at any pool or beach.

Photography Before taking photos of someone, ask – or mime – for approval.

Places of worship Be respectful in sacred places. Remove shoes and dress modestly when visiting temples and mosques.

Health

o Tap water in Bali is never safe to drink.

o Widely available and cheap, bottled water is generally safe but check the seal is intact when purchasing. Look for places that allow you to refill containers, thus cutting down on landfill.

o Most ice in restaurants is fine if it is uniform in size and made at a central plant (standard for big cities and tourist areas). Avoid ice chipped off larger blocks (more common in rural areas).

o Avoid fresh juices outside of tourist restaurants and cafes.

o In south Bali and Ubud there are clinics catering to tourists, and just about any hotel can put you in touch with an English-speaking doctor.

o For serious conditions, foreigners are

best served in the costly private clinic **BIMC** (📞 0361-761263; www. bimcbali.com; Jl Ngurah Rai 100X, Kuta; ⏰ 24hr).

° Unless you are definitely sure that your health coverage at home will cover you in Bali, you should take out travel insurance; bring a copy of the policy as evidence that you're covered. It's a good idea to get a policy that pays for medical evacuation if necessary (which can cost US$100,000). Some policies specifically exclude 'dangerous activities', which can include scuba diving, renting a local motorcycle and even trekking. Be aware that a locally acquired motorcycle licence isn't valid under some policies.

° Traveller's diarrhoea (aka Bali belly) is common. Stay well hydrated – rehydration solutions such as Gastrolyte are the best for this – and if it doesn't improve within 24 hours, consider antibiotics.

° There are ongoing reports of injuries and deaths among tourists and locals due to *arak* (the local spirits that should be distilled from

palm or cane sugar) being adulterated with methanol, a poisonous form of alcohol.

° Although *arak* is a popular drink, it should be avoided outside established restaurants and cafes.

° Bali is hot and humid throughout the year. It normally takes at least two weeks to adapt to the climate. Swelling of the feet and ankles is common, as are muscle cramps caused by excessive sweating. Avoid dehydration and excessive activity in the heat.

Money

ATMs are common and it's easy to exchange money. Credit cards are accepted at more-expensive establishments (but there is often a surcharge of around 3%).

ATMs

There are ATMs all over Bali – most accept nonlocal ATM cards and major credit cards for cash advances.

° Most ATMs return your card after dispensing cash, so it's easy to forget your card.

° Card skimming is a widespread problem in Bali – try to use ATMs attached to banks if possible and keep an eye on your bank balance after making withdrawals.

Moneychangers

° US dollars are by far the easiest currency to exchange. Try to have new US$100 bills.

° Find out the going exchange rate online. Know that anyone offering a better rate or claiming to charge no fees or commissions will need to make a profit through other means.

° Stick to banks, airport exchange counters or large and reputable operations such as the **Central Kuta Money Exchange** (www.central kutabali.com), which has locations across south Bali and Ubud.

Tipping

Restaurants Tipping a set percentage is not expected, but if service is good, 5000Rp or 10%+ is appropriate.

Services Hand cash directly to individuals (drivers, porters, people giving you a massage, bringing you beer etc); 5000Rp to 10,000Rp or 10% to 20% is generous.

Hotels Most midrange and all top-end hotels add 21% to the bill for tax and service.

Public Holidays

Tahun Baru Masehi (New Year's Day) 1 January

Tahun Baru Imlek (Chinese New Year) Late January to early February

Wafat Yesus Kristus (Good Friday) Late March or early April

Hari Buruh (Labour Day) 1 May

Hari Waisak (Buddha's birth, enlightenment and death) May

Kenaikan Yesus Kristus (Ascension of Christ) May

Hari Proklamasi Kemerdekaan (Independence Day) 17 August

Hari Natal (Christmas Day) 25 December

Safe Travel

It's important to note that compared to many places in the world, Bali is fairly safe. There are some hassles from the avari-cious, but most visitors face many more dangers at home. There have been some high-profile cases of visitors being injured or killed on Bali, but in many cases these tragedies have been inflamed by media sensationalism. Boat travel carries risks. Take precautions.

Toilets

o Western-style toilets are almost universally common in tourist areas.

o During the day, look for a cafe or hotel and smile (public toilets only exist at some major sights).

Visas

Visas are easily obtained but can be a hassle if you hope to stay over 30 days.

Responsible Travel

Accommodation & Guides

o Choose hotels with Green Globe certification (www.greenglobe.com).

o Staying at a homestay ensures that that your money goes to locals.

o Dive with instructors who have Reef Check EcoDiver certification.

Minimise Your Footprint

Waste disposal is a huge problem – most rubbish and sewage goes straight into the ocean.

o Don't buy water in plastic bottles – bring a reusable bottle with you.

o Bring biodegradable shampoo and soap.

o Turn off lights and air-con when leaving your room.

o Take up offers not to wash towels and bed linen every day.

o If hiring a motorcycle, source an electric version.

Avoid Animal Cruelty

o Never swim with dolphins caged in an aquarium.

o Don't drink kopi luwak – luwak (civets) are often kept in battery cages and force-fed coffee cherries.

Language

Indonesian, or Bahasa Indonesia as it is known to the locals, is the official language of Indonesia. It has approximately 220 million speakers, although it's the mother tongue for only about 20 million – most people also speak their own indigenous language.

To enhance your trip with a phrasebook, visit lonelyplanet.com.

Basics

Hello.	*Salam.*
Goodbye. (leaving)	*Selamat tinggal.*
Goodbye. (staying)	*Selamat jalan.*
How are you?	*Apa kabar?*
I'm fine, and you?	*Kabar baik, Anda bagaimana?*
Excuse me.	*Permisi.*
Sorry.	*Maaf.*
Please.	*Silahkan.*
Thank you.	*Terima kasih.*
You're welcome.	*Kembali.*
Yes.	*Ya.*
No.	*Tidak.*
Mr/Sir	*Bapak*
Ms/Mrs/Madam	*Ibu*
Miss	*Nona*
What's your name?	*Siapa nama Anda?*
My name is ...	*Nama saya ...*

Do you speak English?
Bisa berbicara Bahasa Inggris?

I don't understand.
Saya tidak mengerti.

Emergencies

Help!	*Tolong saya!*
I'm lost.	*Saya tersesat.*
Leave me alone!	*Jangan ganggu saya!*
Call a doctor!	*Panggil dokter!*
Call the police!	*Panggil polisi!*
I'm ill.	*Saya sakit.*
It hurts here.	*Sakitnya di sini.*
I'm allergic to (antibiotics).	*Saya alergi (antibiotik).*

Numbers

1	*satu*
2	*dua*
3	*tiga*
4	*empat*
5	*lima*
6	*enam*
7	*tujuh*
8	*delapan*
9	*sembilan*
10	*sepuluh*
20	*dua puluh*
30	*tiga puluh*
40	*empat puluh*
50	*lima puluh*
60	*enam puluh*
70	*tujuh puluh*

80	delapan puluh
90	sembilan puluh
100	seratus

Eating & Drinking

What would you recommend?
Apa yang Anda rekomendasikan?

What's in that dish?
Hidangan itu isinya apa?

That was delicious.
Ini enak sekali.

Cheers! *Bersulang!*

Bring the bill/check, please.
Tolong bawa kuitansi.

I don't eat... *Saya tidak makan...*
dairy products
susu dan keju
fish
ikan
(red) meat
daging (merah)
peanuts
kacang tanah
seafood
makanan laut

a table ...	*meja ...*
at (eight) o'clock	*pada jam (delapan)*
for (two) people	*untuk (dua) orang*

Shopping & Services

I'd like to buy ...	*Saya mau beli ...*
I'm just looking.	*Saya lihat-lihat saja.*
May I look at it?	*Boleh saya lihat?*
I don't like it.	*Saya tidak suka.*
How much is it?	*Berapa harganya?*
It's too expensive.	*Itu terlalu mahal.*

Can you lower the price?	*Boleh kurang?*
There's a mistake in the bill	*Ada kesalahan dalam kuitansi ini.*
credit card	*kartu kredit*
foreign exchange office	*kantor penukaran matauang asing*
internet cafe	*warnet*
mobile/cell phone	*henpon*
post office	*kantor pos*
signature	*tanda tangan*
tourist office	*kantor pariwisata*

Transport & Directions

bicycle-rickshaw	*becak*
boat (general)	*kapal*
boat (local)	*perahu*
bus	*bis*
minibus	*bemo*
motorcycle-rickshaw	*bajaj*
motorcycle-taxi	*ojek*
plane	*pesawat*
taxi	*taksi*
I want to go to ...	*Saya mau ke ...*
At what time does it leave?	*Jam berapa berangkat?*
At what time does it arrive ...?	*Jam berapa sampai di ...?*
Does it stop at ...?	*Di ... berhenti?*
What's the next stop?	*Apa nama halte berikutnya?*
Please tell me when we get to ...	*Tolong, beritahu waktu kita sampai di ...*
Please stop here.	*Tolong, berhenti di sini.*

Behind the Scenes

Send Us Your Feedback

We love to hear from travellers – your comments help make our books better. We read every word, and we guarantee that your feedback goes straight to the authors. Visit **lonelyplanet.com/contact** to submit your updates and suggestions.

Note: We may edit, reproduce and incorporate your comments in Lonely Planet products such as guidebooks, websites and digital products, so let us know if you don't want your comments reproduced or your name acknowledged. For a copy of our privacy policy visit lonelyplanet.com/privacy.

MaSovaida's Thanks

Deepest thanks to the wonderful souls who provided assistance, insight and companionship throughout my time on Bali: Rob, Margie, Max, Kristy and the Outsite crew; Gigi and Annette; Ty and Jeff; and especially to my dear brother Bayu for an efficient and unforgettable journey.

Mark's Thanks

Thanks to all the people on Lombok and Sumbawa who steered me in the right direction and helped me to navigate the post-earthquake islands, even when their personal lives were in shambles. I owe a debt of gratitude to Rudy Trekker, Gemma Marjaya, Kelly Goldie and Andy Wheatcroft for being fountains of

This Book

This 7th edition of Lonely Planet's *Pocket Bali* guidebook was curated by MaSovaida Morgan, and researched and written by MaSovaida, Mark Johanson and Virginia Maxwell. The same team researched and wrote the 6th edition. The 5th edition was curated by Imogen Bannister, and researched and written by Ryan Ver Berkmoes. This guidebook was produced by the following:

Destination Editors Niamh O'Brien, Tanya Parker

Senior Product Editors Kate Chapman, Amy Lynch

Product Editors Pete Cruttenden, Amanda Williamson

Senior Cartographers Alison Lyall, Julie Sheridan

Book Designers/Cover Researchers Fergal Condon, Wibowo Rusli

Assisting Editors Imogen Bannister, Melanie Dankel, Carly Hall, Lou McGregor, Sarah Stewart, Simon Williamson

Thanks to Carolyn Boicos, Roland de Vries, Chris Dixon, Grace Dobell, Bruce Evans, James Hardy, Gunilla Jäghagen, Bella Kane, Anne Mason, Ambika Shree, Lyahna Spencer

knowledge along the way. A special thanks to my partner Felipe Bascuñán for tolerating my long absences and to my editor Niamh O'Brien for tirelessly ensuring I was OK!

Virginia's Thanks

Thanks to Ryan Ver Berkmoes for the Bali briefing, Hanafi Dharma for the expert driving and navigation, and Niamh O'Brien for monitoring the safety situation. My support team of Peter and Max Handsaker stayed calm when they saw the earthquake reports and made regular Skype calls to check up on me. I couldn't work as a travel writer without them.

Acknowledgements

Cover photograph: Pura Luhur Ulu Watu, R.M. Nunes / Getty Images ©

Photograph p30: Aaron Lim / Shutterstock ©

Photographs p31: (left) randi_ang / Shutterstock ©; (right) tims images.uk / Shutterstock ©

Index

See also separate subindexes for:

⊗ **Eating p158**

🍷 **Drinking p159**

✪ **Entertainment p159**

🔒 **Shopping p159**

Our Writers

MaSovaida Morgan

MaSovaida is a travel writer and multimedia storyteller whose wanderlust has taken her to more than 40 countries and all seven continents. Previously, she was Lonely Planet's Destination Editor for South America and Antarctica for four years and worked as an editor for newspapers and NGOs in the Middle East and United Kingdom. Follow her on Instagram @MaSovaida.

Mark Johanson

Mark grew up in Virginia, USA and has called five different countries home over the past decade, while circling the globe reporting for British newspapers (*Guardian*), American magazines (*Men's Journal*) and global media outlets (CNN, BBC). When not on the road, you'll find him gazing at the Andes from his current home in Santiago, Chile. Follow the adventures at www.markjohanson.com

Virginia Maxwell

Based in Australia, Virginia spends at least half of the year updating Lonely Planet destinations across the globe. The Mediterranean is her major area of interest but she also covers Finland, Bali, Armenia, the Netherlands, the US and Australia. Follow her @maxwellvirginia on Instagram and Twitter.

Published by Lonely Planet Global Limited
CRN 554153
7th edition – Apr 2022
ISBN 978 1 78868 377 7
© Lonely Planet 2022 Photographs © as indicated 2022
10 9 8 7 6 5 4 3 2 1
Printed in Malaysia